When Your
Children
Divorce

ELAINE R. SEPPA

INTERVARSITY PRESS
DOWNERS GROVE, ILLINOIS 60515

OVERTON MEMORIAL LIBRARY
HERITAGE CHRISTIAN UNIVERSITY
P.O. Box HCU
Florence, Alabama 35630

©1995 by Elaine R. Seppa

All rights reserved. No part of this book may be reproduced in any form without written permission from InterVarsity Press, P.O. Box 1400, Downers Grove, IL 60515.

InterVarsity Press® is the book-publishing division of InterVarsity Christian Fellowship®, a student movement active on campus at hundreds of universities, colleges and schools of nursing in the United States of America, and a member movement of the International Fellowship of Evangelical Students. For information about local and regional activities, write Public Relations Dept., InterVarsity Christian Fellowship, 6400 Schroeder Rd., P.O. Box 7895, Madison, WI 53707-7895.

All Scripture quotations, unless otherwise indicated, are taken from the HOLY BIBLE, NEW INTERNATIONAL VERSION®. NIV®. Copyright ©1973, 1978, 1984 by International Bible Society. Used by permission of Zondervan Publishing House. All rights reserved.

ISBN 0-8308-1644-5

Printed in the United States of America ♾

Library of Congress Cataloging-in-Publication Data

Seppa, Elaine R., 1922-
    When your children divorce/Elaine R. Seppa.
        p.   cm.
    Includes bibliographical references.
    ISBN 0-8308-1644-5
    1. Divorced people—Family relationships. 2. Parent and adult
    child. 3. Divorce—Religious aspects—Christianity. I. Title.
HQ814.S427 1995
306.874—dc20   94-45526
                                                                    CIP

| 18 | 17 | 16 | 15 | 14 | 13 | 12 | 11 | 10 | 9 | 8 | 7 | 6 | 5 | 4 | 3 | 2 | 1 |

| 09 | 08 | 07 | 06 | 05 | 04 | 03 | 02 | 01 | 00 | 99 | 98 | 97 | 96 | 95 |

To my husband, Karl,
and our four children, who have
continued to meet
the challenges of family life both in
good times and in crises
with courage, love and mutual support.

To Bill and Helen Lower
who helped formulate the dream and
continued to support me as I completed the book.

Foreword

Christians are usually caught flat-footed by divorce.

While church people accept that Christians are not immune to the ravages of our culture on the family, it is still a shock to deal with divorce in the families of your own children. Parents discover that it's not only their children's hopes and dreams that die. Their own dreams die as well.

So there is a great need for this book. When Elaine Seppa and her friend Helen Lower asked me years ago for resources to help parents of adult children going through divorce, I had to admit there was very little available. When divorce strikes, all the academic studies and sermonic exhortations seem of little use. Even close friends often don't know how to help. I urged Elaine to write about her own experiences and the resources she was discovering.

She had to look only as far as our own church to discover many people willing to share experiences of divorce in Christian families. Dozens of the families in the church were still dealing with hidden feelings of recrimination, self-accusation and disappointment. These were couples who had weathered storms in their own marriages. They weren't perfect parents, to be sure, but could they really have failed so dismally in passing their convictions on to their children? They wondered why their children seemed to give up so quickly on the ideals which they—and the church—had fostered.

Elaine probed those feelings. She heard the deep desire of parents to restore communication and trust with their children. *When Your Children Divorce* is the result of her work. It comes not only from her own experience but from her careful listening to many others and from her deepening awareness of spiritual resources available through Christ and his church. This book offers forthright, honest and perceptive help to families who have found divorce thrust on them.

Elaine recalls the early emotions of anger and guilt, the turmoil of not knowing how to help, the embarrassment she felt when she spoke to friends about her children's divorces. You will feel her strength as you consider questions you thought you would never have to answer: How does a mother-in-law relate to the ex-spouse? Who is to be included in family celebrations? What does one do with all the resentment one feels because of what has been lost forever? This book is rooted in reality.

The book's uniqueness, however, is in the authentic hope it offers. The final chapters describe a spiritual journey marked by a closer walk with Christ, a deep calm, and trust in the God who "restores all things." Our spiritual journey is connected to our physical and emotional life. Through "the fellowship of suffering" connected with divorce, Elaine finds integration that centers on God's active involvement in her situation.

Elaine tells distressed parents, "Your responsibility is to represent the grace and forgiveness of God in the midst of very imperfect circumstances." To do that herself, she was forced back to experiencing afresh God's grace and forgiveness.

Her spiritual journey is not a self-conscious theme. It just undergirds all she says, giving extraordinary depth and power to the way she deals with crisis or allows the crisis to affect her. In this book, as in her life, you will see the marks of a maturing disciple of Christ dealing with events and emotions that tear people apart. Yet she remains whole and can tell the story with humility and insight.

I wish I could have written this book. It says what I have long wanted to say, and it is going to minster to many more people than the mothers and fathers who are anxious over their sons and daughters. There is, for example, an excellent chapter on how fathers and grandfathers deal with the divorces of their children. There are chapters on maintaining relationships with grandchildren and on dealing with all the complex relationships remarriage brings. I especially appreciated the chapter on how the church can uphold marriage and yet offer compassion and practical care to struggling couples.

Is God still God when divorce occurs? With *When Your Children Divorce,* individuals and churches need no longer be caught off guard about either the risks of divorce or the redeeming grace of God.

Steve Hayner
President, InterVarsity Christian Fellowship

Acknowledgments

During the time it took for this book to come into being, many people contributed to it. They offered personal encouragement, confidence in the value of the work and in me, stories from their own individual and family pilgrimages, editorial direction, and prayer support during my own quest for perspective. Pastors, therapists and others shared their professional insights. I am truly thankful for all who have been part of this supportive network.

Steve Hayner, then our pastor, who had faith in Laura and me and challenged us to write this book.

My husband, Karl, who has continually believed in me and encouraged me, joyfully taking on extra tasks and providing equipment so that I could write.

My two sons whose stories were the impetus behind this book. They have encouraged me and released me to write; I am ever grateful for their trust.

My two former daughters-in-law, who were able to trust me with this story.

All four of our children, who lived the events, felt the pain, and learned the lessons—and who celebrate the result.

Lee Dale, who believed that I could learn to use a computer, patiently teaching me on his own machine when I didn't even know how to type.

Dottie Dale, my partner in counseling ministry and prayer partner for twenty-five years, who has loved, supported and encouraged me throughout this writing.

The couples and individuals who shared their personal

stories. Though their real names are not used in the book, their stories are very real. Special thanks to "Sydney," who shared hers in moving detail.

Sue Lockett John, my writing coach, who helped me refine my skills and critiqued my work with love. She believed in the book—and in the process has become a true friend.

My small group Bible study, who were such good listeners: Hazel Larson, Muriel Watson, Doxie Hogue and Adelle Scarvie.

Our couples' support group, who for ten years shared their lives with Karl and me—learning to listen to one another and to seek after God: Dick and Donna Grout, George and Vonnie Dickson, Helen and Harold Sternberg, and Lee and Dottie Dale.

My Monday morning Bible study group, women who upheld our family and my writing project until its completion.

My P.E.O. sisters (dedicated to education for women), who believed in me and provided continuing enthusiastic support.

Mary Worthington and David Van Liew, in whose class I learned to expand my understanding of creativity and explored the possibility of writing this book. A new world opened to me, and I am truly grateful.

Bruce Larson, who as my pastor encouraged me to risk and "dream the impossible dream."

Earl F. Palmer, my current pastor and friend, whose words of affirmation and belief in the book propelled me to continue seeking a publisher and led me to InterVarsity Press.

Linda Doll, my editor at IVP, who graciously guided this neophyte writer through the process of refining the manuscript, believing it could have a ministry. She has been a delight.

Numerous dear friends, most of whom I met when they were college students and came to our home, who watched me move through the slough of despond to stand on the bank and find a path forward—loving me all the while.

1

The Shocking News

●

"MOM, THINGS ARE not good. Our marriage is falling apart."

Stunned, I held my breath and clutched the phone while our daughter-in-law tried to explain that she loved Tim but was no longer *in* love with him. I felt numb, fearful to speak—I might say the wrong thing and somehow make matters worse. *This can't be happening!*

After a few agonizing days a letter arrived from Tim, our second son, devastated by the pain of hearing his wife say, "It's over." He affirmed his love for us and his need to be in close touch in the midst of his confusion. When I read his letter, I finally could weep and release the solid knot of agony that had been growing inside of me. Nothing in our life as a family had brought such pain. The months ahead would be filled with tumultuous change and would demand honest evaluation of our long-held beliefs and values.

When our four children became adults, Karl and I thought our parenting work was behind us. We had done everything we knew to give a foundation for a meaningful life. We had nurtured them and taught them values based on our Christian faith, which we both had held since childhood. We had helped them obtain an education. We saw them choose marriage partners whom we came to love. We saw them establish themselves in their chosen professions and enjoy fulfillment with their own families. Now we were enjoying them as friends and had set them free to realize their own dreams.

We had not looked for signs of trouble in our children's marriages. This son and his wife had been married for fourteen years and had often talked about how good their marriage was. They felt a responsibility to share their home and family life with others. So Karl and I were completely unprepared for the crushing news we were now hearing.

Separation and divorce proceedings followed within the year. All of us experienced a deep sense of loss and, at times, overwhelming sadness. We grieved. Our dreams for our son and daughter-in-law's happiness and for our continuity as a family were shattered.

Further Pain

Three years later the second shoe dropped. Our older son, Steve, arrived with his children at a family work party. Their mother had some things to do at home and was unable to join us. We all enjoyed the day, helping one another, not suspecting what was to come that evening.

"Mom, we need to talk. Can we go for a walk?" I felt a flash of foreboding as Steve and I walked to the park across the street. I learned that his marriage, too, was now seriously threatened. He and Becky were separating. How could this be happening *again* in our close, loving Christian family? It seemed as if I was hearing about complete strangers.

The numbness was back.

Karl and I learned that divorce has become almost as common among Christian families as among non-Christian ones. It is estimated that approximately 50 percent of all first-time marriages end in divorce. We have four children—we had reached the average!

Our sons' divorces devastated my husband and me. We never expected such a thing in *our* family, so we were taken completely off guard. How could we handle our emotions? What should we do—with relation to our son, our ex-daughter-in-law, our grandchildren, but also regarding our own daily lives? Everything was different; everything was confused.

Months seemed to drag by. The Bible and prayer were real comforts to me, assuring me of God's love, but I also needed specific help to process my questions. I searched the libraries and bookstores but found nothing dealing with the pain felt by parents of divorcing individuals, from either a Christian or a secular point of view. A couple of books have appeared more recently, but the main writing in this field focuses on the divorcing couple and their children. Little notice is given to parents, grandparents, siblings, brothers- and sisters-in-law, and other relatives whose family dynamics also are fractured. There is a special need for material for Christians, whose fundamental beliefs about God's love and God's laws are called into question.

Looking for Help

I went to Laura, a friend of many years, whose son had divorced several years before. From the outside, this marriage had appeared to be "made in heaven" and tied with a large bow. I knew the divorce had been very painful for her and her husband. I asked Laura, "When you were searching for answers, did you find books or other resources that I have overlooked?" Her answer was no.

Though a measure of healing had taken place for her, she was willing to revisit the memories, not only to help me but to consider what might be done to help others as well.

Together we went to our pastor, Steve Hayner. He knew both of our families well and had watched us process our pain. He said firmly, "I believe there is a real need for a book for folks in your situation—and the two of you should write it!"

Writing in my journal that night (July 9, 1987), I recognized several levels of feeling. One was a sense of excitement at Steve's confidence in both of us and in our gifts that complement each other: Laura's organizational ability and my counseling skills. Then there was a sense of joy that yes, I believe this is God's call to us, and Steve's affirmation and encouragement confirmed it for me. And there was a sense of adventure underneath, as I realized that this new "calling" might be similar to the time when Dottie (my prayer counseling partner) and I began teaching classes and workshops on inner healing: step by step God has walked with us through an incredible journey of growing faith and counseling ministry for more than twenty years. Finally, there was a feeling of awe about what would come to pass in the next months as Laura and I tackled this project that God was setting before us.

At Steve's urging we began the process of writing a book directed to parents and families whose lives are directly or indirectly influenced by divorce among their adult children. (Our numbers, unfortunately, are increasing in the Christian community.)

We began our quest for deeper understanding by being very vulnerable with each other. We opened our personal journals that had been written during the time of our children's divorces. We talked of our grief, told our personal stories. We had so many questions. As we shared more deeply with our husbands and then with other Christian couples, we discovered common threads of experience and confusion. In different ways we all had asked: "We feel so helpless; what can we do to help in this situation?" "We're so angry. How could they do this to us?" "Do you suppose he/she is having an affair?" "Do you think they would go for counseling? Could we help them with it financially?" "Has this happened because of something that we did or didn't do?" "This is wrong, isn't it?" "What will the church and our friends think?" "What will happen to our grandchildren?" "What about responsibility and commitment—is this the *new way* for couples to solve their problems?"

Laura and I worked together for several months, going beyond our own experiences, talking to many people. We first interviewed twenty-five parents whose children were divorced or in the process of divorce. Most of the interviews were with couples and were taped. We also talked with many other people who found out what we were doing and wanted to share their stories.

As the idea of the book began to take shape, we saw the need to talk with pastors and priests from many denominations. They proved very willing to share their experiences and describe their churches' policies.

It was important to get input from marriage and family counselors, particularly regarding the hard realities of abuse and its impact on family life. I talked with ten counselors.

We completed our study by sending questionnaires to workshops sponsored by Divorce Recovery, receiving thirty returns from divorced individuals.

As we read and talked with people, we searched for common themes, for ideas that would be helpful for other parents as well as ourselves. Then Laura was unable to continue with the book, putting it aside because of the demands of full-time employment. However, the book contains significant portions of her story and her research as well as mine.

I found healing in this process of research and writing. It forced me to look at my attitudes and responses, to compare others' viewpoints and experiences, to become aware of a much broader picture than I had previously known. As a Christian, I struggled to reconcile the biblical passages that say divorce is wrong with our unconditional love for our children and our belief in a God of grace and forgiveness. It became a quest for understanding and growth.

Isn't Divorce Wrong?

Please do not think this is a book recommending divorce. I believe divorce is the breaking of a marriage covenant that was made before God. Every divorce is tragic and regrettable. It creates widespread pain. Like the other broken relationships in our lives, it reflects our very human condition.

I also believe that God, in his love and mercy, forgives us when honest confession is made and forgiveness is sought. He is a God of restoration and new beginnings. That does not mean that we can take divorce lightly. It does mean that our Lord refuses to cast people out on the ash heap when we sin. He still loves, and he will forgive and restore.

As parents, Karl and I realized we needed to cease judging our children (that is God's job) and to start expressing God's unconditional love day by day. Forgiving our children was a part of what was required of us. We had to stop focusing on what used to be; we had to focus on the future and the ways in which God could redeem what sin and human weakness had brought about.

This book was not written to prove divorce right or wrong.

I begin my story and the story of others at the moment when parents learn of their children's decision to divorce. It is written to give you support and perspective, to help you recognize and process the changes that come crashing into your life, ready or not.

Not Our Decision

The divorce of our son Tim and his wife was followed by that of our older son, Steve, and his wife. Both times Karl and I wrestled with guilt—were we in some way the cause of the tragedy?

In the process, we realized that the decision to divorce was made by our children, not by us. We didn't like the decision, but we were not given a vote. Our children were adults, making their own choices now. Few of the parents whom I interviewed had the opportunity to directly influence their children's decision concerning divorce. They most often learned about it after the fact, then had to cope with the consequences.

So guilt was not the proper response. Instead, our challenge was, *How does God want us to express forgiveness, love and compassion in this undesirable set of circumstances?*

There are steps you can take and tools that will enable you to move away from sadness, anger, blame and unforgiveness, toward healing and restored relationships. This book doesn't offer a how-to. I share personal perspectives but also reflections and insights from other Christian parents. We must each follow our own quest, find our own way through the tangle of emotions and circumstances.

Several divorced individuals have told me that they had no idea how widely the ripples of their divorce would extend. The experiences shared through these pages are also meant to provide insight and perspective for extended family members and friends where divorce is being considered or has become a reality.

In most cases I have used pseudonyms to protect the privacy of parents and adult children. Many of the stories I have shared contain essential elements common to more than one set of parents, and all are painfully true.

There Is Hope

At the time of this writing I have experienced much healing, although the road is not always smooth. There are still stabs of pain in one form or another, but I see growth in Karl and myself and in our children.

As I observe our sons and grandchildren developing strength and resilience these days, I am very grateful to God for his faithfulness in the midst of trouble—and for the promise that as we seek his face, he will continue to work in all our lives to bring about wholeness.

2

"I Feel Ashamed and Guilty"

•

I WAS STANDING AT the kitchen sink holding a glass measuring cup in my hand as I looked out on my garden. Wanting to have my hands free, I crammed the cup into the garbage disposal and flipped the switch! I listened. It jammed at first, then slowly started its labored, noisy grinding. Shards of glass began spinning out in every direction. Impulsively I swept these back into the disposal with my bare hands. It gr-r-round on.

I awakened with a start, appalled!

Later I had vivid recall of this dream that had troubled me the night before. Dreams frequently give me insight into my inner state of mind. As I pondered, understanding began to come. In the wake of my son's separation, I was feeling just like that cup—*shattered,* flying in all directions. What had been whole was now in pieces. Shards of pain, fear, anger and sadness pierced my being.

I felt engulfed in powerlessness, sorrow, fear about the immediate future, pain over broken expectations and dreams. Most other parents with whom I talked told of the same confusion in their reactions. "These emotions don't seem to follow a logical pattern; they just keep happening over and over," said one mother. Yet most parents experience the same erratic cycles of emotion.

Even if you have known your child's marriage was seriously threatened, you may be surprised at your reaction when it finally breaks apart. Sometimes there is a double set of emotions: relief on the one hand, sadness and disappointment on the other. Take comfort in knowing that you aren't the only one who has felt these feelings.

Laura remembers trying to describe her agony by saying that she hurt from the top of her head to the tips of her toes. Her prayer was, *Dear God, why? Why does it hurt so terribly?* Her sense of loss and betrayal was severe.

She told me: "I remember thinking back twenty-five years to when I lay in my hospital bed with my newborn son in my arms. What a miracle he was! Perfect. Just as God had meant him to be. And as I touched each part of that tiny, trusting body, I envisioned the future. What would he be, this helpless tyke? Whose would he be? I believed that my son would know God's counsel and find happiness and success in that. Looking back now, I realize it's not that simple."

Why do we parents suffer when our children divorce? Laura commented, "As Christians, we want God's best for ourselves and for those we love. We believe his best is community—in marriage, that means committing to a lifetime with a husband or wife. When that commitment is broken, we know there will be scars.

"When we have watched our child's marriage relationship

grow and have bonded closely with our child's mate, it's doubly painful to see it die. When it does, our hopes and desires for their future—and ours—as part of a close-knit family die with it.

"Most of us believe that ugly things happen only when parents don't care, when they don't pray and don't participate in the lives of their kids. I was naive. There are no guarantees! Through my son's divorce I realized that the time had come for me to become more mature in Christ, to grow up as a Christian in a mucky world. God doesn't *cause* this to happen in families, but he says, 'Since this choice has been made, my child, let me teach you some things you have not yet discovered about yourself, about life and about me.' "

Pride Causes Pain

If we're honest, we will admit that part of our pain comes from pride. When our children get divorced, our prideful image of ourselves as good parents is threatened. We have diligently reared our sons and daughters the best way we know how. Many of us have struggled with the prideful assumption that we are responsible for our children's choices. Divorce forces us to question whether there was something that we did or did not do that indirectly contributed to the problem.

It's particularly painful if too much of our identity is wrapped up in seeing our children as extensions of ourselves. Their academic achievements, creative expression and athletic prowess add to our sense of worth. "You're so-and-so's parents, aren't you? You must be proud of him!" Our children's achievements and successes affect the whole family. Sometimes we depend too much on those for our own sense of self-esteem.

The reverse is also true. We actually *feel* our children's failures, and sometimes we feel judged because of them. Nevertheless, when they are grown we must try to step back and expand our perspective. Their choices are their own, made in the midst of their particular circumstances. Genesis 2:24 declares that "a man will leave his father and mother and be united to his wife." When our sons and daughters marry, we recognize their new, separate identity as a couple, a new family unit. If that marriage succeeds, it's their success and we can rejoice. If it fails, we must accept that reality and move on, being as supportive as we are able.

Our pride is confronted when we face people outside the family circle—our friends whose children's marriages have not failed. How hard it is to say, "Dick and Jane have separated."

Margery told me of encountering old friends at church. "We hadn't seen each other for a few months, and their greeting was warm. They naturally asked how the children were. Tears suddenly filled my eyes. I gave some lame excuse and left them standing there while I made a hasty exit. I felt unreasonably angry at them for not knowing the children had divorced. I wasn't sure how they would respond to the truth. My pride was hurt. I identified with what I considered my children's failure. I was torn between exposing my pain and just muddling along. I'd hoped that somehow others would find out so I wouldn't have to say anything. Even more, I had hoped that the decision to divorce would be reversed."

It's even harder to expose the truth about a marriage breakdown when you and your children are perceived as leaders and are always expected to succeed. In such circumstances you may be tempted to avoid being with people you know—making vague excuses, not participating in the usual activities—while you work through your injured pride.

However, as one father, a pastor, said, "There is merit in enduring a 'goldfish bowl' situation." During his child's marital turmoil and subsequent divorce, it had not been easy or comfortable to realize that "everyone in the church observed the conflict and knew that the kids were having serious trouble." The surprising thing was that friends didn't take sides. Instead they made every effort to keep in touch with all parties involved, and the church became a supportive extended family. This was particularly helpful for the divorcing couple's children, who didn't have to experience separation from their friends because of divided loyalties.

With hindsight, the father of the divorcing husband realized that "the only way to be real in the face of crisis is to let people know how you are feeling instead of trying to 'be cool,' 'keep a stiff upper lip' or 'go it alone.' " He and his wife had to lay aside their pride, their expectations and their need for their children's marriages to be perfect. This couple began to see that the failed marriage was not their failure but the result of their children's decisions and behaviors.

Guilt Causes Pain

In my response to our sons' divorces I frequently asked myself these questions:

□ What did we do wrong while our children were growing up?

□ How did we contribute to the problems that brought about the divorce?

□ Were we inaccessible when they asked for help?

□ Did we smother them or negate their independence with our advice?

□ Did we listen?

□ Did we have unrealistic expectations, wanting our children to be perfect? Did this cause conflict between them?

□ Did we give them a healthy model to enable them to learn from their mistakes, seek forgiveness and go on?

□ How do we need to grow?

I told myself that I should have seen what was happening and been more sensitive and available. I was able to help others who came to me for counseling but not my own loved ones. (They hadn't sought my help; at first I felt guilty even about *that*.)

It is easy to assume the guilt for what our children do. Some of us believe that we must be perfect parents who have reared perfect children. It starts when they are small and other parents frown at our sweet little ones when they misbehave, as though to say, "My, my, those parents haven't done a very good job." We feel guilty. We want them to be perfectly behaved, bolstering our own ego. An initial reaction to the news of divorce, then, may be much the same. We feel guilty. But what are we guilty of? Of falling short as a parent? Too little love? Too protective? Too permissive? Unrealistic expectations? Too little affirmation to build their confidence? Perhaps we should never have allowed the marriage to take place!

Of course we have fallen short as parents. There are no perfect parents and never will be. But the thoughts go round and round. Does anyone really know the answer?

These questions and many more come pouring out of parents' mouths as they share the effect of guilt on their lives after the divorce of a son or daughter—especially when all the fingers point to *their* child as the one who is to blame.

Two Kinds of Guilt

One couple, Joe and Maria, recalled feeling guilty and deeply angry with themselves. Joe mentioned, "I was reminded of what I was unable to give this child as his father." Maria interrupted, "No, it's really my fault because I wasn't a good enough mother." She tearfully recalled holding her tiny grandchild whose parents had recently divorced. "It was many months before I could rock this baby to sleep without crying. I wished this baby were my own son and that I could start over again and do it right this time."

It is important to discern between the two kinds of guilt: true guilt that results from sin, and false guilt that says, "I should have made everything work out perfectly."

When working through feelings of guilt, we first have to realize that all parents make mistakes. We have all failed—and will fail—our kids. There may have been times when we were selfish and insensitive in the instructions and rules we laid down. Or sometimes we were poor listeners and even drove our kids away from us. To the extent that we may have sinned against them, our guilt is true guilt, and we need to ask God's forgiveness. He does forgive—and he removes that sin, so it no longer deserves any place in our minds. Accepting the truth that God forgives and is able to redeem our mistakes is a giant step in the process of healing.

Once we determine what we are truly guilty of—indiscretion, judging, pride—we can confess it honestly to our Father. God doesn't want us to wear masks. He wants us to be ourselves when we come to him in prayer. When we keep communication clear with him, we are free to be ourselves and to be his agents of love in the midst of troublesome or perplexing circumstances.

Sometimes I get discouraged because I'm bringing the same things to God over and over in my times with him. The things that I don't want to do I do, and the things that I want to do I fail to do (Rom 7:15-21). We all struggle with this. But we are to come to our heavenly Father with our failures, our true feelings and our questions. He knows that we are weak, so he has provided a way to take care of it—through prayer.

Maria and Joe gradually learned to be less harsh with themselves, to put what they perceived as their own failure behind them and, having asked God's forgiveness for any wrongdoing, to forgive themselves. What was done was done. It was history. Maria sought family counseling to understand her own behavior patterns and began the healing process by first acknowledging some real failure and taking steps to correct it. She and Joe, being people of faith, could accept

God's forgiveness—it was forgiving themselves that was more difficult.

If you find it difficult to believe that God has really forgiven you, you may find it helpful to ask your pastor to listen as you pray for forgiveness, then to pronounce forgiveness in the name of Christ, on the basis of God's promise.

The other half of dealing with true guilt is going to those we have offended. If we have done things that were hurtful to our children, or if we have failed to do things that would have helped, it is important to go to them and ask for their forgiveness. Then we should seek to make amends if at all possible.

But much of our guilt regarding a divorce in the family may be false guilt. It is important to realize that *we are not responsible for our child's divorce.* How could I have been responsible for the choices that my grown children had made in the daily living of their lives? I lived hundreds of miles away, and months went by between visits. They weren't asking our advice, and we weren't giving it. My false guilt was wrapped up in my expectations of them and of my parental role. Laura was right when she told me, "Even being perfect parents (if we could) wouldn't guarantee the success of our children's marriages."

My pastor helped relieve my false guilt with his counsel: "Most of us parents do the best we know how, but we all are imperfect. We give what we can. We share our values, our belief in Jesus and our purpose in life. We may take our children to Sunday school and have devotions in the home, but as they reach their late teens and become adults, we must let them go to make their own choices. We should neither own their sins nor claim their victories. We are not responsible for either the good things or the bad things that they choose."

King David knew a lot about guilt. After he was confronted, he confessed it flat out—on his face before God. He anguished and cried. In Psalm 38:4 he said, "My guilt has overwhelmed me like a burden too heavy to bear." In Psalm 40:1-3 he tells us, "I waited patiently for the LORD; he turned to me and heard my cry. He lifted me out of the slimy pit, out of the mud and mire; he set my feet on a rock and gave me a firm place to stand." And then the bonus: "He put a new song in my mouth, a hymn of praise of our God."

Freedom Follows Forgiveness

David knew that with God there was forgiveness. We too need to realize this very good news; so do our children. "If we confess our sins [just tell him what is really going on in our minds and hearts], he . . . will forgive us our sins and purify us from all unrighteousness" (1 Jn 1:9). David pleaded with the Lord: "Create in me a pure heart, O God, and renew a steadfast spirit within me. . . . Grant me a willing spirit" (Ps 51:10, 12).

What will it mean to have "a willing spirit"? It will mean taking time to honestly look at yourself, to find out what you are feeling. It will mean coming before God in quietness and honesty, willing to listen to him as you ask, "What is it, Father, that you want to teach me about myself in this situation?"

Instead, we're more apt to protest:

☐ "I have so much work to do now that I can hardly keep my head above water. I don't have time to think about how I feel."

☐ "I'm afraid to look at myself and see guilt, judging or pride."

☐ "I have to concentrate on the task at hand."

I've learned to ask myself this: *Do I want to be whole and free?* We are instructed to come before God and confess our sin (anything that keeps us from full relationship with him). Preoccupation with our children's divorces can cloud our interactions with God. I've learned that when I am willing to look at myself and accept the fact that I have failed in some areas, and then talk to God about it, together we can get things straightened out. He offers his forgiveness and cleansing. Then I am free and am given the courage to take the action that needs to be taken. Then I am able to live each day in a more effective way, as he puts a new song in my mouth.

3

"I'm Angry, Worried and Afraid"

●

TANGLED WITH THE pain of a child's divorce is anger. It can be overwhelming. You may feel a helpless rage that turns your stomach and goes beyond anything you have ever felt before. Reactions to anger differ: Some parents lash out, some withdraw, others fret and stew.

"I wanted to put him over my knee and spank him!" John told me when I asked him how he felt about his son's divorce.

George, another angry and disappointed father, sputtered, "Young people have a strange idea about how to solve their problems these days."

Aili, whose daughter had divorced nine years before, was still burning with anger. She said, "Our daughter was left to care for two children, one with Down syndrome. Her husband used up all their money and manipulated and lied to everyone. I don't care if I ever see him again—I don't *want* ever to see him again!"

One couple was furious because their lives were interrupted. They had had the perfect family. Everything ran smoothly and looked beautiful. Now they were ashamed and embarrassed: their wide circle of friends would see that all was not as perfect as it had appeared. Unable to face working through their feelings with others, they withdrew from the friends who loved them.

Laura was angry that her son had ignored her in his decision to divorce. She sensed that he had made the decision in his own heart and mind without consulting anyone—not a counselor, not his wife, not God and certainly not his mother! Her anger was similar to what she had felt during his growing-up years when he had disobeyed her or ignored her advice. She cried, "I want him to see me as a person to whom he can come to share his hurts—a person who can console, counsel, perhaps show him some avenues that he can walk down that may (or may not, I'm open to that, I think!) lead to healing the breach. Was I such a terrible mom in the past that he can't see me in that role?"

Anger can be intertwined with protectiveness—for yourself (*I don't want my life to be interrupted!*), for your child (*How could he do this to my daughter?*) and perhaps most of all for your grandchildren, especially if your child has been left with the burden of childrearing.

Jane and Chris were furious because their daughter moved out and left their son-in-law to care for two young children. "If the adults want to blow their lives apart it's one thing, but what about their beautiful children?" exploded Chris. Long phone conversations produced only superficial discussion and no additional understanding. "We've just grown apart" was the excuse.

Understanding Anger

It's difficult to identify and accept feelings of anger. Most of us aren't used to dealing with our feelings openly, especially the negative ones. It's uncomfortable. Some Christians believe that we aren't supposed to be angry, so they deny such feelings.

In *The Angry Book*, Theodore Rubin says,

We may have heard and been conditioned by statements like: "If you get angry, I'll know that you don't love me." "Nice boys and girls don't get angry." "If you get angry at least be polite." "If you get angry you'll get into trouble," etc. A healthy emotional environment exists where all kinds of feelings are accepted openly and freely without threat of reprisal. In this environment no feeling or expression is labeled "good" or "bad." An unhealthy environment exists in which people often feel one way but act another. When they are angry, they smile sweetly or freeze and do nothing at all.1

Tight control creates the illusion that our anger is gone, but it can fester and surge up, exposing itself when we least expect it. Rather than deny what we feel, we need to understand our angry response and what has brought it about.

The emotion of anger is amoral, neither good nor bad. It is a God-given emotional response, just like joy or sorrow. My emotions are not open to judgment. It's what I do, inwardly and outwardly, with my emotions that is open to judgment.

Michael Rogers, a friend who is a Christian counselor, helped me to better understand the biblical teaching about anger. He pointed out:

There are several places in the New Testament where Jesus was angry or where anger was acknowledged. Ephesians 4:26 (RSV) says, "Be angry but do not sin; do not let the sun go down on your anger." So clearly there is anger that is not sinful. The issue is what we do with our anger when it arises.

When some of our basic needs (love, pleasure, belonging, security, creativity) are unmet, we respond by being *hurt*. Time passes, we continue to remember the hurt, and anger flares as a response. Now what do we do with the anger? One option is to confess it and ask God to increase his love in us, helping us to act in accordance with his will. We may need to communicate with the person or persons involved and take some specific action concerning the issue at stake.

Up to this point we have expressed anger, our God-given emotion. If nothing changes, we continue to remember the hurt and allow it to fester. The anger turns to resentment. The focus has now changed from the issue to the person or persons who caused the hurt. Resentment grows into bitterness; then the next step in the progression is fury, or rage. Rage simmers and grows into hatred; then revenge and even murder may follow. "See to it that no one misses the grace of God and that no bitter root grows up to cause trouble and defile many" (Heb 12:15). Anger attacks the issue, but rage attacks the person. Anger is an ally while rage is our enemy—it is destructive.

Anger is a secondary emotion. It can be defined as "a hurt remembered" or "a response to a violation." It is important to understand why we are hurt, so that we can act responsibly. Anger becomes sinful when it festers (when it's not processed toward and through the hurt) and becomes rage.[2]

Our response to this emotion is what is important. The tendency is to direct it at someone—attacking (usually verbally) the person we perceive to be at fault. We may call names, blame others or commit violence. That is far from healthy. It is far from being Christlike.

We can ask God to help us move in constructive ways. But even with his help it is a struggle sometimes. Seven years have passed since the first divorce in our family, and occasionally I still feel flashes of anger. My interviews with other parents tell me that I am not alone.

Handling Our Anger

Beth took some steps toward healing. First, she was able to say, bluntly but honestly, "I know I'm angry, and it hurts like hell." Second, she talked to trusted friends and allowed her anger to escape, like steam from a pressure cooker. Third, she listened to tapes—both music and teaching—which renewed her mind with something worthwhile and uplifting. She worked at letting go, an ongoing process.

King David is a good example of how to process negative emotions. In the Psalms he continually vents his feelings. He cries out his fears, vindictiveness and despair, and calls upon God to take care of his enemies. In passages such as Psalm 143:4-10 (RSV) we watch him work through his emotions until he becomes able to bless God or express gratitude for God's faithfulness:

Therefore my spirit faints within me;
    my heart within me is appalled.
I remember the days of old,
    I meditate on all that thou hast done;
    I muse on what thy hands have wrought.
I stretch out my hands to thee;
    my soul thirsts for thee like a parched land.
Make haste to answer me, O LORD!
    My spirit fails!
Hide not thy face from me,
    lest I be like those who go down to the Pit.
Let me hear in the morning of thy steadfast love,
    for in thee I put my trust.

37

Teach me the way I should go,
   for to thee I lift up my soul.
Deliver me, O LORD, from my enemies!
   I have fled to thee for refuge!
Teach me to do thy will,
   for thou art my God!
Let thy good spirit lead me
   on a level path!

How can we acknowledge our anger and channel it in meaningful directions? Many of us erupt when we hear that our children are divorcing. We would like to respond rationally from the outset, but we can't control our initial response. The reaction just comes—bang! Later we have time to think about it—and perhaps to regret it.

But as we begin to adjust to the news, we can choose our responses. Our emotions are like our motor—they propel us to act. Our rational ability can be the steering wheel that determines the direction of this action.

Choices

Choose not to let the anger eat you up or permanently damage your relationships. Watch out for destructive responses:

☐ Don't immediately jump on the bandwagon and start blaming your child's spouse, especially in front of grandchildren. Your anger may be justified, but carelessly expressed anger can wound deeply. Be quick to listen and slow to speak.

☐ Don't continue to let your mind spin in downward circles, asking yourself, "What did he do?" "What did she do?" "Why didn't they . . . ?"

☐ Don't take over and try to straighten things out. Let these adult children live their own lives.

☐ Don't try to explain one spouse's behavior to the other one when you don't really know the whole story.

Use your anger as an ally to propel you to accomplish

something constructive. This energy can become a creative expression.

☐ Exercise. Exercise allows you to let off steam physically. It defuses stress and helps you relax. It will get your heart and lungs in better shape. Walking can provide time to meditate on the beauty around you and recognize that God is present as a resource.

☐ Clean! More than one woman has said that her home was cleaner during this angry period than at most other times. Drawers and closets got organized too. Or you might pump this energy into digging vigorously as you plant a garden, pounding nails in a woodworking project, pummeling the dough as you prepare to bake bread.

☐ Talk to a friend. Let some of the intensity of your emotions escape. You may need to talk to your pastor. Gain some fresh perspective. It is not necessary, and not healthy, to bear this alone. If your children's decisions are not yet public, explain to them that, while you will be discreet, you will need to tell one or two trusted friends who can help you work through your own shock and pain.

☐ Inform yourself. Get some books about divorce and related subjects. Find out what resources are available. Is there a Christian Conciliation Service in your area that might help your children define and work through disputed issues?

☐ Do something for someone. We don't always have control over the events that affect our lives, but we can choose not to focus only on those events. It may be something as simple as helping a neighbor do a task or preparing a "care package" for a friend, or it may involve getting more deeply involved in ministry to others.

☐ Write about your feelings. Journaling may help you become aware of what you are feeling and thinking. Then you can choose to take responsibility for the feelings and do something about them. If you can't journal, write letters to your child expressing your feelings—writing can help drain off the accusation and hurt—but don't mail the letters and add needlessly to your child's pain. Destroy them as a ritual (literally burning them can become a "burnt offering" to the Lord) and let the feelings go.

☐ Pursue a hobby. As a beginning weaver, I've found that getting absorbed in a weaving project where my mind and hands are both fully engaged is very relaxing and beneficial. I forget the pain for a time and am refreshed.

☐ Pray. Prayer can keep our focus off the pain and on God and his presence and power. I often pray and walk at the same time. It helps sometimes to write down in my journal where those prayer walks have taken me:

> When I pray for insight it usually comes. . . . What came through loud and clear today was that there was a "lust for power to control the circumstances."
>
> It surprised me, and then I began to see all the ways I have needed to have control. Several areas were quickly evident, one being the children's decisions ending in divorce. I spent some time recommitting these areas and asking for the Lord to fill my spirit with love and truth and for his counsel to replace my pride and controlling attitudes. I feel lighter in my spirit and am thankful that he, Jesus Christ, is more than adequate to work his loving ways—I don't need to wear myself out playing "supermom" or "almost God."

Begin your prayer by asking for God's protection so that the thoughts that come to you are from him. You don't need to use formal words. You are in conversation with your Lord, and you need only to talk to him about what you think and feel and the guidance that you need. Then slow down, be quiet and listen so that he can speak to you through your thoughts. It's a good idea to check what you perceive to be his guidance against Scripture, to see if it rings true with Jesus' instructions to his people. Remember that when you are a believer in Jesus, the Holy Spirit is within you to be your teacher and counselor, and he will guide your thoughts.

Fear and Worry

Medical research has made us aware that stress takes its toll on our bodies and our emotions. Because of this, my husband and I feared for our personal health as well as the future of our children and grandchildren. At one point I was so distraught that I thought, "I could have a stroke." Karl's stomach ulcer, long dormant, began to give him distress. We took steps to get regular exercise, maintain good nutrition and reduce the stressors as much as possible. It was important to remain healthy!

The major worry, not only for me but for many of those with whom I talked, was: How will divorce affect the lives of our grandchildren in the months and years to come? It was easy to focus on the negative side of that question. But what did I gain by fretting about what the future *might* hold for these innocent victims of divorce? Nothing! Someone has aptly said, "Worry is like rocking in a rocking chair. It gives you something to do, but you don't get anywhere."

I also worried that what I said, or might say, out of love and concern would not be heard in the way that it was intended— that there would be a breakdown in communication, fracturing the loving relationship of many years.

When we feel strongly and our emotions are running high, we tend to speak before we think through the message we want to impart. We may make pronouncements or accusations that backfire instead of conveying the love that motivates our words. Our message may sound unloving or even hateful. A friend gave me some important advice when I was thinking up angry speeches toward my son and daughter-in-law: "Be careful, Elaine, not to say something that you will regret." I'm not sure that I always succeeded, but I realized careless words were a luxury I could not afford.

And what happens when you know, the minute you say it, that something is causing pain, and you wish you could take it back? Instead of lying awake all night worrying, talk to the Lord about it and then make a plan to call or write the person you have hurt. Honestly state your regrets and try to explain your motivation. Perhaps time will be on your side and, as you find ways to demonstrate your love and commitment, the hurt of those words will fade.

We can't control our reactions; we *can* control our responses. Lloyd Ogilvie says that "so many of the things we regret in the expression of our impatience [fears] are caused by reacting before we have prayed for the mind of Christ."[3]

Saint Paul says, "Do not be anxious about anything, but in everything, by prayer and petition, with thanksgiving, present your requests to God. And the peace of God, which transcends all understanding, will guard your hearts and your minds in Christ Jesus" (Phil 4:6-7). Further on in the same chapter he says, "And my God will meet all your needs according to his glorious riches in Christ Jesus" (v. 19).

Psalm 4:8 says, "I will lie down and sleep in peace, for you alone, O LORD, make me dwell in safety."

We don't and can't know what the future will bring. However, today, you and I can bring our fears and worries, our guilt, anger and pain before a loving God who cares for those hurting people you and I love so much. How many times the words of Scripture have been a source of reassurance, release and direction to me when I was worried and fearful. Jesus says, in John 14:27, "Peace I leave with you; my peace I give you. I do not give to you as the world gives. Do not let your hearts be troubled and do not be afraid." And Saint Paul writes, to encourage both Timothy and us, "For God did not give us a spirit of timidity, but a spirit of power, of love and of self-discipline" (2 Tim 1:7).

These and many other passages of Scripture remind us of God's promises to us who believe in him. Our children and their welfare are also his concern. He can guide and influence our thoughts, lead us to resources and bring alongside us those who can help us. Our God is able!

4

But It's Time to Move On

•

OUR SON'S DIVORCE was final. I struggled to adjust to the reality of it. A significant relationship within our family had changed abruptly. I was left feeling shaken, powerless and disoriented. Karl and I didn't know what to expect, now, when we planned a family gathering or a visit to our son. I felt awkward and tense because new people were filling roles formerly held by others. Even some of our friendships had changed. Uncertainty swirled around me every day. Yet I had to get out of bed each morning and continue living my life.

During this period I read Eugene Peterson's helpful book *Run with the Horses*.[1] His chapter titled "Letter to the Exiles" tells of Israel's being exiled to the land of Babylon, the violent uprooting of a people from their homeland. The Israelites' response to their new surroundings seemed all too familiar.

Like them, I was filled with fear, self-pity and rebellion. I had been uprooted from the patterns and rituals of family life that we had built over a period of almost twenty years. Words such as *separation, divorce, hearing, settlement, child support, joint custody* felt like a foreign language and were unacceptable when applied to *our* family. Yet they were becoming a part of our everyday vocabulary. I was in exile!

The Blessing of Ordinary Tasks

Jeremiah the prophet had written to the exiled Israelites with God's instructions of how to live in Babylon. He told them, "Build houses and settle down; plant gardens and eat what they produce. Marry and have sons and daughters. . . . Seek the peace and prosperity of the city to which I have carried you into exile. Pray to the LORD for it, because if it prospers, you too will prosper" (Jer 29:5-7).

In other words, go about the business of ordinary life: plant a garden and enjoy the harvest, marry and have children. Do what you would normally do despite these unexpected—unwanted—changes in your life. As I read, I wondered, *Can I benefit from Jeremiah's instructions to the Israelites? Would it help me if I again did some of the creative activities I'd done in the past?*

I realized that I too must concentrate on the joy of daily tasks and routines. I needed to keep on watering my plants. I needed to be fully and joyfully involved with the family celebrations and festivals. Peterson says, "The aim of the person of faith is to live as deeply and as thoroughly as possible—to deal with the reality of life, discover truth, create beauty, act out of love. Exile forces decision."[2]

Each day brought me the opportunity to examine some of my long-held opinions and preferences and to discard those that had little value in living the Christian life. I could decide to live as best I could with these circumstances. I could choose to act out of love rather than out of my disapproval or my hurt.

But how could I "seek the peace and prosperity" of the people who were the sources of my hurt? Two daughters-in-law whose decisions I grieved over and whom I didn't want to lose; two sons whose loneliness pierced my heart; later, the new women they brought into our family; the new family units my daughters-in-law established, which included replacements for my sons—how to pray sincerely for these people to prosper? The answer to that question came more slowly. I had to decide to stop blaming, accept the new realities and pray for the family's welfare.

Taking Care of Yourself

During this time I often journaled while sitting in my great-grandmother's rocker in the sunny corner of our bedroom. Her immigrant trunk, which carried her family's belongings from Switzerland to the New World in 1871, sits alongside the rocker. A comforting presence, it reminded me that I come from tough stock. Somehow it was easier to face the hard days, choices and transitions when I could pour out my feelings in a place where I sensed family solidarity and continuity. Here in my corner I could quietly reflect, explore my attitudes and open my inner self to God's creative ideas.

I encourage you to find a quiet corner somewhere too. Provide soothing music, a favorite afghan and a cup of tea for yourself. If solitude is not possible at home, perhaps you can drive to a small park nearby and just sit in the car looking at the trees. Try to relax the tightness in your body and your soul. Then your mind and emotions will be able to flex as you think through the demands, and perhaps opportunities, of your new circumstances.

Looking back to where I had been and forward to where I needed to go, I could see life as a process. Laura told me something she had discovered: "My present pain is only a small part of the total span of life." I began to lift my eyes beyond my current circumstances to consider the future. The long-range view helped me begin to cope more realistically with the present reality. I started to make decisions about where I would focus my attention and time.

The Point of Decision

As I've heard how others have healed from the trauma and pain of their children's divorces, I've realized that they too reached a point of decision, a time when they realized, *I can choose how I will respond to difficulty and to people who have caused me pain.* Many couples told me: "I made the decision to accept the fact that things were going to be different—and to love, no matter what. But along with that, I made the decision not to give my child the power to spoil my life."

I believe such a decision is crucial for resolution and healing. We are able to make such a decision when we are at the "rock bottom" of the experience of exile.

The following list of turning points was given to me by one of the women I interviewed. She told me that she wrote it to remind herself of the decisions she had made about how she was going to respond to her undesirable circumstances. I include her list, with her permission, because it models the sorts of realizations which can help you heal from the pain of a child's divorce.

❑ I have determined that I am not going to let myself be torn apart by one child.

❑ I am not going to concentrate on the problem that is existing in the family because of one divorce.

❑ I am going to spend more time praising God for the three families that are intact.

❑ I have made a conscious choice not to get bogged down on who he was, who she was, what we could have done. It is too easy to concentrate on the negative.

☐ I made the decision that I could not expect things to be the same now. I had seen my family as a whole pie, but now a wedge had been taken out. I decided that this did not spoil the whole pie, it just made it different.

Another parent told me, "I came to the point where I had to decide for health and happiness rather than sickness and sorrow. Once the decision was made, my direction changed. Some big walls fell down when I decided that I could not—and should not—be responsible for the actions of another person. I don't have to try to change them or to make it right. It's simply not my responsibility."

Get Support

It's difficult to make these decisions alone. God made us for community. We need to surround ourselves with family members and friends who can listen, clarify our feelings and reactions, gently point out discrepancies in our thinking.

If you do not have a supportive spouse sharing this journey with you, support from a few other people you can trust will be all the more crucial. Don't be afraid to ask for it. Being a part of a small group where personal sharing is part of the focus—and where confidentiality is an absolute—can be most helpful. (See chapter ten on small groups.) Seek out those people and decide to concentrate on positive growth. Attending a "Change and Transition" or "Families in Crisis" class may bring knowledge of resources and a helpful perspective. Counseling services or churches may offer such classes.

Avoid Big Changes

A word of caution: When you are in the midst of turmoil, space out the stressors, if possible. Try not to make major changes like changing your residence or taking on heavy organizational responsibilities. When we are in a chaotic state, we're off balance and need to concentrate on the simple routines of day-to-day living.

The tasks of housekeeping and pursuit of familiar activities afforded me new pleasure as I lived with the emotional turmoil. One counselor's advice was, "Be gentle with yourself; don't make additional, strenuous demands on your time and emotions. Cutting yourself off from the normal and predictable routines can add to your stress."

Accepting What Is

As I struggled to accept my son's divorce, I remembered my own efforts several years earlier to bring perspective to my mother. She was in her mid-seventies and was suffering emotionally because one of her grandsons had taken up wine-making as a new hobby. All her life she had held to an unshakable code of behavior that strictly forbade any use of alcohol, and now she intended to "cut off all contact" with this grandson.

I had written in my journal,

Today as she was spouting again about his rebellion against her values, I reminded her that Jesus was very vocal about the sins of the heart: hypocrisy, greed, self-righteousness, lack of love and compassion. Behavior that came as a result was far more critical than what went into a man's stomach. I reminded her that if she followed through with her threat to "have nothing more to do with him," she would lose her influence in his life about the things that were important to her. We talked some about this and then nothing more was said.

I heard no more from her about the wine-making and neither did the grandson. (Interestingly, this grandson showed consistent love and concern toward my mother throughout her aging years.)

As I remembered this episode, it struck me that I had been reacting in much the same way toward my son's divorce and some of the changes in his values. I saw the cross-generational legacy of judgment and self-righteousness that had been modeled for me. I didn't like it, but it was a lesson I needed to learn. Acceptance allows us to move toward reconciliation and balance.

For me acceptance meant several things:

☐ The divorce was a reality.

☐ I had to come to grips with the everyday changes that resulted. At family gatherings our conversations were guarded, because no one wanted to bring up painful topics. Sadness sometimes clouded the atmosphere.

☐ After two sons' wives had left our family circle, my remaining daughter-in-law and I missed them. We missed the fun and companionship that "we girls" had enjoyed, planning for future gatherings or giggling over something that had happened.

☐ I had to recognize and believe that God's love is an enabling resource. Some days I could feel it; some days I could not.

☐ I needed to explore how this situation could be an opportunity to learn and to draw closer to my family.

Accepting Our Inability to Change Someone Else

Some of the parents I interviewed talked about how hard it is to accept their adult children's adoption of values and lifestyles that don't match their Christian values. If you are facing this, I urge you to realize (sometimes it takes a while) that love doesn't call us to change our adult children or "fix" them. It calls us to support and love them in good times and bad.

When we observe our children's problems, we may have a knee-jerk response and start "acting like parents" again. We may be tempted to shield ourselves from the truth or to reassume responsibility and start giving *unsolicited* advice. Don't do it! Acceptance means letting them bear responsibility for their own decisions.

Facing Our Need to Forgive

Another side of acceptance may be a harder assignment: we need to forgive our children. Earlier I discussed our need to forgive ourselves for our mistakes as parents. We also need to forgive others.

Sandra D. Wilson says, "It is impossible to fully reach for hopeful tomorrows with both hands full of yesterday's resentments and regrets. Therefore in our journey to shame-free living and parenting, we need to release those resentments and regrets about 'what might have been' so we can embrace the reality of what is and pursue the potential of what can be."[3]

When each divorce hit my family, I had a choice to make. Would I choose to release and forgive what seemed to me to be a cover-up, lack of wisdom, seeming disregard of the consequences for their children—and on and on? Would I forgive each son for his part in the marriage failure? Would I forgive my daughters-in-law? I could stand in my judge's robe and be miserable—or I could choose to forgive, as God (who had forgiven me for so much) was asking me to do.

Facing Our Need to Be Forgiven

At the news of the first divorce, for a short time the sorrow caused me to retreat into myself and partially withdraw from my husband, my most obvious source of comfort. I just couldn't talk about this terrible thing. But I needed to share my feelings, and so did Karl. When I realized this, I saw that my sulky silence did not honor God's power to bring good out of the situation or out of the chaos that I felt. I needed to seek Karl's forgiveness.

David Augsburger explains, "Forgiveness recognizes what has really happened, owns the hurt incurred, responds to the other person with integrity, and affirms new behavior for the future with genuine intentions."[4] That was the kind of forgiveness I needed (and received) from Karl.

My journal recalls it this way and shows the power of gaining awareness and asking and receiving forgiveness:

I went to put some good music on the stereo and gradually the heaviness and anger left me. I could prepare lunch, and then I could ask Karl's forgiveness, owning that "I must be hard to live with right now. I feel so very vulnerable." The silence is gone between us, and I feel God has heard my prayers.

Heavenly Father, I know that when I am honest with myself and you about my feelings, that is the first step for you to begin to heal me with your love and forgiveness. Obedience brings peace . . . you are King of kings and Lord of lords. If you keep the galaxies running in perfect balance, surely you are able to help us with our lives and the living of each day.

For each of us there comes a challenge to grow or to remain stuck in our feelings. We have the power to decide and act! Accept the fact that neither you nor your children are perfect, that the divorce is real. God calls us to be transparent, so don't be afraid to be honest with yourself about how you feel.

Forgive yourself, your children and others who may be involved. Ask forgiveness, if necessary—from God, from your mate, from anyone else who hangs heavy on your mind.

Forgiveness is at the heart of Jesus' message. God does not withhold forgiveness. But how can we receive forgiveness from God if our hands are closed like fists and we are refusing to give forgiveness to others? Peter Kreeft likens our unforgiveness to the Dead Sea, which receives living water from the River Jordan but, because there is no outlet, becomes salty and unable to support life. Contrast this with the Sea of Galilee, which receives fresh water, supports an abundant fishery and releases fresh water. Kreeft says, "If we dam up love's exit river to our neighbor [family], we also dam up love's entrance river from God."[5]

If we continue to hold grudges, we make it possible for the "root of bitterness" talked about in Hebrews 12:15 to grow, and we'll miss the grace of God. Jesus commands us to forgive, but we are free to choose to obey or disobey.

The cost of disobedience is high. We often feel the effects of unforgiveness physically as well as emotionally and spiritually. The tension from unforgiveness builds up in us and we suffer from headaches, weariness, stomach aches, ulcers and so on.

Barriers to Forgiveness

No one can tell another person when it's realistic to forgive. You must make that choice yourself, when your heart is ready. How do you know when you're ready? When you're tired enough of the pain and anger that you are willing to set aside your "rights" and take the risk. Forgiveness, like love, is not just a feeling; it is an act of the will.

It helps to recognize some of the barriers to seeking forgiveness:

❑ We want the other person to come and ask us for forgiveness. After all, their action caused us pain. (Forgive for your own sake and in obedience to God; don't wait for apologies.)

❑ We lack honesty with God about our true feelings: we feel our anger is justified and don't want to let go of the resentments we feel. (If you aren't willing to forgive, then you need to ask God to help you be willing. If you remove your mask and reveal your hurts and feelings to him, he will help you change.)

❑ We are afraid that by forgiving someone we open ourselves to being hurt again by that person. (Forgive anyway, and live in reliance on God's protection.)

Several times I was sure that I had forgiven and had ceased being angry, only to come to the realization that there was still more hurt and anger. I needed to go back again and again and ask God's spirit to show me the truth about myself. Then I needed to listen to his reply.

With God's unlimited resource of love, I am able to forgive and find peace. It does not happen immediately. *Forgiveness is not an event but a process.* It takes time. It takes perspective.

Julie shared her story one morning:

My small study group had met for years, looking to the Bible as well as other books for inspiration and practical understanding for life. We also spent time sharing our concerns—both personal and broader ones. These friends observed how miserable I was over the divorce that had occurred in our family. Sure, I had made adjustments and kept busy. But I had been miserable for years—blaming, judgmental and unforgiving. Yes, I was a Christian—one in need of repair.

One day it suddenly seemed very clear. It was *my* attitude that had to change! I was the one who was keeping the family separated into camps. I was still looking backward, at what used to be. I needed to move beyond that habit and make an effort to get the whole family, with its new additions, together. I would never know what healing might take place until I tried.

I asked for help: "Father, give me courage to do what I'm beginning to understand is part of your will—to open my mind to your possibilities in this circumstance. Help me open my heart too, instead of continuing to think *I* have to do it all, so that you can equip me with your resources. I haven't been able to do it on my own. But your Word tells me 'nothing is impossible with God' [Lk 1:37]. Help me embrace your promise."

I will never forget the look of joy on the faces of all my family as they gathered in my home to prepare and share a meal. I had thought it was impossible. I'm on cloud nine and I hope I never come down!

Unless forgiveness comes from a willing heart, it simply is not real, nor is it enough. Make the decision to forgive; ask God to help. He has given you the resources already—you just have to draw on them. In so doing, you free yourself to move on to meet the circumstances as they arise, without the burden of unresolved feelings.

The Phillips translation of Ephesians 4:31 says it this way: "Let there be no more resentment, no anger or temper, no more violent assertiveness, no more slander and no more malicious remarks. Be kind to each other, be understanding. Be as ready to forgive others as God for Christ's sake has forgiven you."

The Scriptures leave little doubt about what we are to do as believers in Jesus. I'll long remember a statement I heard pastor and teacher Tim Dearborn make: "God doesn't ask us to do something that he is unwilling to equip us to carry out. He will work in us to help us be *willing* and then *able* to forgive, if it is the desire of our heart."

5

"How Can I
Help My
Hurting Child?"

●

A LIFETIME OF PARENTING cannot prepare us for all the challenges we will face when our children divorce. In the midst of the emotional turmoil, there is a very strong desire to help. We would like to reduce our children's pain and help in practical ways. But we don't know how.

We are called to play a supportive role, in the very best sense of the word. The divorced men and women I talked with expressed an overwhelming desire for acceptance, unconditional love, understanding and support while they found their way. Everyone's circumstances are different, though, and helpful responses to those needs may differ.

While writing this book, I asked divorcing men and women how their parents' responses to their divorce affected them. I submitted questionnaires to Divorce Recovery Workshops, which serve three to four hundred people each year. Here are some of their answers.

☐ "I had no idea what the ripple effect of my divorce would be."

☐ "Why are my parents so upset? It's my problem, not theirs."

☐ "When my parents moved closer so they could 'help with things,' I felt that the independence I sought for myself and my children was compromised. I guess it didn't hurt, but it didn't help either."

☐ "I wished my parents wouldn't immediately jump on the bandwagon to blame my spouse, because I carried some responsibility for the breakup."

☐ "I want to be treated like an adult, not a child. I didn't need them to fix it!"

☐ "I wanted to know I still had a place at home." (This son moved back home for a few weeks while he sorted things out.)

☐ "I needed for them to be open to listen nonjudgmentally. To hear me out."

☐ "I wanted my father to be vulnerable and share his true feelings. His distance kept me off balance." (Several expressed their longing for honest reactions, not superficial ones.)

☐ "Is it ever appropriate to withhold information to protect them? I was so aware of their pain."

☐ "I urged my parents to obtain counseling to help them gain better understanding. They didn't take my advice, and I feel their agony was prolonged."

Saying It Right

Sometimes divorcing young people have an unrealistic view of their parents' concern for their well-being. As parents, we continue to have concern for our children no matter how old they get. But young people may resist this, at least until they are very secure in their own identity.

For example, many parents are still cautioning their children to "drive safely" long after they are grown. If a friend says, "Well, take it easy over the pass," no offense is taken. But if a parent says that, it may sound to the adult child like, "You aren't able to take care of yourself yet; you still need my instructions." We help our children most when we relate to them as responsible adults.

When divorce threatens, is it any wonder that parents verbalize concern for their child's marriage, make judgments, become fearful and sometimes express anger? Yet their concern should be expressed in ways that support and don't undermine or destroy their relationships with their children, who may be struggling with damaged egos already. As parents, we can work at expressing our concern on an adult-to-adult level and not with scolding or overprotective adult-to-little-child words.

The Proper Distance

Even children who once considered their relationship with their parents open and communicative sometimes find that divorce causes the relationship to deteriorate. Parents may find it very difficult to be present where angry words fill the air and conflict is acted out. So we may avoid visiting our children. This distancing on the part of parents, particularly fathers, makes it harder for some children to cope.

In other families, the troubled couple may feel "this is our problem" and may push parents and in-laws away. Yet in other cases parents find they are being asked to become more involved.

Perhaps we have only recently learned how to let our married children live their own lives, how to enjoy them from an appropriate distance. Now we must find a way to be supportive without returning to parenting patterns of the past. We can offer comfort, provide emotional and practical support, challenge our children with responsible behavior. We can listen as well as give leadership. We can seek and offer forgiveness. But we must not try to live their lives for them.

Playing a Supportive Role

Because we love them, we want to reduce our children's pain. Sometimes in our zeal to see harmony restored we may step in to "fix things." Perhaps we have always responded this way to our child's dilemmas. We may have been the mom who repeatedly ran to school with the forgotten lunch or the dad who could be counted on to deliver the papers when it rained.

We may feel pressure from well-meaning family or friends who imply, "He [she] is your kid, you'd better make things right." Trying to "make things right" may prove to be toxic. It takes wisdom to act constructively. Remember, in this particular play we are not the stars. We are part of the supporting cast. When we forget that, tensions grow.

We may be called upon primarily to fulfill the roles of listener, caregiver/provider and intercessor.

The Role of Listener

In my survey of men and women who had divorced, the one thing they most desired was a parent who would *listen*. It isn't always easy to be a good listener, particularly when we feel that our child has made some very poor choices and now is experiencing the consequences. Regardless, we are called to try to hear in love, even though we may not always agree.

When the news of divorce is unexpected and unwanted, listening to your child can be particularly challenging. However, your child needs someone to hear the anguished "Why?" or the desperate "I can't go on," to hear the anger and hurt, the fears for the future and even the outbursts of vindictiveness and blame.

A good listener allows the speaker to talk through the

situation, then reflects back what has been said in order to clarify the original thought. Perhaps you need to say, "I'm not sure I understood what you just said—did you mean . . . ?" A good listener suggests additional or alternative conclusions without telling the other person what to do. You might say, "Have you already considered . . . ?" But definitely avoid saying, "What you need to do is . . . !"

Good listeners allow the speaker to get something off his or her chest, to "blow off steam" and not have it taken as the final word on the subject. Many times the speaker is just throwing out ideas to hear how they sound and has not formed solid conclusions yet. Let him or her finish. If we are too quick to jump in with our answers or comments, communication stops.

It is a privilege to have children of any age feel safe enough with us to pour out their hearts. Some parents long for that opportunity but never have the chance.

A word of caution: I'm not saying that you should be available to listen at any time, day or night, or for any amount of time. You may need to clarify when you are available to listen. Or, if the exchange is not constructive, you may need to end the conversation. Circumstances will help you find the balance between supporting your child and sacrificing yourself.

I had to learn how to set boundaries, how to support my sons and also care for my needs. Late phone calls sometimes set my thoughts churning endlessly. Until I learned how to change my focus before going to bed, I was unable to sleep. It helped me to listen to some good music or read something that refocused and engaged my mind. Then I needed to pray and commit my child and the circumstances, and also my own sleep and rest, to the refreshment of God's peace and control. Often your child will appreciate your setting guidelines in order to care for yourself; you can say, "Unless you really need to, could you try not to call me after nine p.m.? I want to talk to you, but I sleep better if we talk earlier." The child then has permission to call and yet knows what times are not helpful for you.

The Role of Caregiver/Provider

John and Pat automatically said yes when their daughter asked to move back home with her two young children. Their daughter's husband had walked out, leaving her without financial support, and she had no immediate prospects of a job.

This couple once again became active parents. But the circumstances were entirely different now. The daughter expected to have many of the privileges of being the child in the family but none of the responsibilities. She came and went as she pleased. She had been doing that for a long time—ever since she had first moved out of her parents' home. Now she expected her parents to take charge of her children while she went out hunting for a job and reestablishing her social contacts.

The parents discovered that, for a period, their daughter experienced "the crazies"! That may be a new term to you, as it was to me, but the definition is easy to understand. It is a period in which many newly divorced people seem irrationally driven to make up for lost time—seeking dates, socializing continually in sometimes uncharacteristic ways, not wanting to be alone, sometimes throwing inhibitions to the wind. It seems to be a frenetic period of busyness, a search for acceptance of their new status, for establishment of a new identity.

John and Pat said, "We had to continually bite our tongues to keep from saying things that would build resentment." However, because they loved their daughter, they worked hard at improving their communicating skills, verbalizing their expectations, choosing to help her and their grandchildren through this difficult period in their lives.

The daughter eventually found a job and moved out on her own. She adjusted her expectations of her parents to more realistic and mutual standards. Now she has remarried and the parents are enjoying their opportunities to grandparent in a more traditional situation.

If your adult child seeks refuge in your home in the initial stages of separation and divorce, it may be easy for you to respond with open arms. One father expressed joy in being able to care for his son in this way but was also free to say, "After a few weeks the atmosphere in our home became so sad and heavy that it was very difficult to continue." Before you agree to be a long-term provider, some very practical issues need to be talked about, first with your spouse and others who may be in the home, and then with your child. *Resentments build up when we are unwilling to verbalize our expectations.*

Here are some of the issues that you might wish to discuss:

☐ Will your child help with the household expenses?

☐ If there are small children, will you offer child care? Under what circumstances?

☐ Are you free to discipline your grandchildren? Will you be expected to do so? One wise parent told her daughter, "I will discipline the children when they are in my care, but when you are present they're your responsibility."

☐ How can you get breaks during periods of prolonged stress?

☐ Does your child need financial assistance? It might be a one-time gift with no strings attached. You might prefer to give a monthly stipend to ease the stress until things settle down. Another possibility might be a one-time loan with a written agreement that clearly spells out the terms of repayment and interest rates. You might wish to set things up so that payments are made directly to your bank. This businesslike approach will be less emotional for everyone.

☐ Could you provide apartment rental if it's not possible to have your child and possibly his or her children in your home?

☐ While your child is in your home, will he or she be expected to help with the household chores? If so, decide which ones: yard work, meal preparation, laundry, cleaning, grocery shopping and so on. Or will he or she come and go without a care or sense of responsibility for the household?

☐ Is the invitation to stay with you open-ended? Plan to evaluate the arrangement in three weeks, six weeks, six months.

These suggestions may seem to be mechanical and unnecessary, but it's much easier to identify possible areas of tension and discuss your expectations *before* problems arise and resentments begin to build.

Other children in the family, even if they have their own homes, may feel jealous of the time, attention and money that they suspect you are spending on this child. They might feel that you are being taken advantage of and want to protect you. It may be prudent to have some conversation to address their concerns and questions.

In a chapter titled "Money, Money, Money" in *What to Do When Your Son or Daughter Divorces,* the authors point out: "At divorce time, money can be a boon or a bust, a bone of contention or a pipe of peace. Your decisions are not made in a vacuum. Your children's eyes are watching, even if they are a thousand miles away. The main issues for you are what your divorcer needs, what you have, whether he or she warrants your help, and what you want to give. One thing is sure, you will agree that money matters."[1] This book offers a very complete discussion of money matters with excellent background and suggestions. It's a helpful resource.

The Role of Intercessor
Our God is God of the present as well as the past and the

future. He loves us and is interested in and actively involved with our lives and the lives of our children and grandchildren. He seeks an ongoing relationship with us all; he wants a wholesome and meaningful life for us, based upon his principles. One of the most important privileges that we have as parents or friends is to intercede in prayer for those we love.

As we think of these loved ones and feel joyous, thankful, troubled or powerless, we can bring them before our heavenly Father, who knows all about the situation and cares far more than we can imagine. He has limitless power to affect circumstances.

It is important to remember that he has given each of us free will to make choices. He will not go against the will of any individual because of someone else's prayers (even when you have prayed for what you are convinced is best for that person).

Sometimes we grow impatient or discouraged when we have prayed but don't see the change we desire. God's timing may be very different from ours—and he doesn't promise to explain it to us! We know too that God doesn't always work in ways we can recognize—so he may be "answering" though we see nothing happening at all.

Some of us are fixers by temperament: when something is broken or out of place, we want to rush in and *get it working right*. It's hard to let go of it and just entrust it to God. But when it comes to fixing other people's lives, that is often exactly what we're called to do.

Parents want those they love to be free from pain, but growth often comes through brokenness. (Why do we and our children often have to endure so much pain and misery before we are ready to seek God's help?) It is in committing our concerns to the Lord in intercessory prayer that we find peace, knowing how very much God loves our children, that he isn't finished with them and will continue to work to bring good out of every circumstance that is committed to him.

You may find that God answers your prayer for a change in your child's behavior by changing your own heart and giving you the courage to forgive or to share your love if you've been unable to do so in the past. You may find you are able to be transparent instead of holding unspoken resentments. And that may prove to be the first element in a gradual process of change in your child's attitudes or behavior.

We will not always see results from our intercession. Yet it is the most valuable thing we can do to help our children.

6

What About the Ex-Spouse—and the *New* One?

●

"DEAR ELAINE." I realized just how much our relationship had changed when I opened a letter from my former daughter-in-law in which she addressed me by my first name instead of "Mom," as she always had. It had taken me a long time to understand what it meant to be a mother-in-law. Gradually it had become part of my identity. Now I experienced a temporary loss of self-confidence. Who was I now to this woman I had come to love?

I was unsure about what each of my two former daughters-in-law wanted from me. Our relationship—what had connected us during these years—had shifted. I felt like the beads of an abacus: pushed up and down, back and forth. Sometimes my sorrow turned to deep anger at divorce and its impact on all our lives.

I missed both of my daughters-in-law, whom I loved deeply. Both of them had been companions whose friendship I valued. I had learned from them about openness, personal honesty and creative expression. Each one helped me to stay younger, more flexible and more aware of our changing world. I loved and appreciated who they were, their talents and gifts.

It was our remaining daughter-in-law, our third son's wife, who helped me see how important it was to try to stay involved with these women who had meant so much to me. It was hard to trust our level of love and believe that it could survive this storm. I had many internal debates; lots of tears were shed. I wanted a relationship that was mutual, but in all honesty it was hard to start the repair work.

I was pleased when Karl and I received a Christmas card from one daughter-in-law that began that process. She wrote on it:

We haven't had much communication, but at this time— celebrating the birth of Jesus—I'd like to experience a rebirth in relationship with both of you. I want you to know that I love you, want to know you and care for you, ask your forgiveness and offer you mine. I wish you and all the family love and peace in the coming year. I hope for a renewed sense of relationship with all of you.

This note brought hope, but it was also hard to receive. The hurts were still so fresh. But God is in the rebuilding business, and I knew I could count on him to help me move into the future. My letter in response tried to honestly express where I was and not gloss over my distress.

You are in my thoughts a great deal—almost daily in fact— as I pray for you and the girls. I have push-pull feelings at times, trying to understand the events of the past months and desiring to move along with what is instead of what was. Thank you for your expression of love and forgiveness. I offered mine before, and I have not withdrawn that. I hope that we can have personal conversation soon, perhaps when you are in town next time, so that we can explore together what our expectations are.

I signed my name "Elaine" instead of "Mom," following her lead, and realized the change was permanent. There is no going back—just ahead.

Grief

When separation and divorce struck our son Steve, his former wife decided to teach school in Europe. She was taking their elder child with her. Our son would have the younger one with him for the school year. Did they ask our opinion? Certainly not! A journal entry:

It has been so hard to say goodby to _____ [our granddaughter] as she leaves with her mother to go to Europe for the school year. We went last weekend for a visit. It was painful to observe Steve being wrenched by this upcoming first-time separation. He will miss her terribly, besides having to experience being a single parent to _____ [their son] for this school year.

Next year the children would change places. This was the implementation of the joint custody agreement.

There were several similar goodbys. Sometimes we felt welcome to be a part of them, but it didn't seem to get much easier. We knew that the children would be separated for the school year, so they would not be experiencing adventures together or be able to support each other. We were heartsick to have our family pulled apart and have no input in the decision.

For several years this former daughter-in-law lived overseas. The first few months I didn't have answers to my letters, but I continued to write some bit of family news occasionally. It seemed important to keep these letters light and to convey that we were trying to understand. It was a long time—or so it seemed to me—before she answered me. But when her letter came, I learned that she had not known whether anyone cared anymore, and she was thankful for my notes. Because of geographical distance, our opportunity to see one another was limited, but Karl and I were grateful for any chance that came along.

No single event in our family's life brought more emotional turmoil than the divorces of our children. In many ways the feelings were similar to those experienced after a death in the family. But with the death of a marriage, we couldn't complete the grieving and move on. Family events continually reminded us of what used to be.

We know the ground rules when there is a death: visiting hours, funeral, sympathy cards and so on. But there are no ground rules to guide us when there is a divorce. It brings a time of uncertainty, grief and change in family relationships. Sometimes these relationships have been established for years and need to be reevaluated so new guidelines can be set in light of the changes.

What About Loyalty?

While in the process of redefining our relationships with our former daughters-in-law, Karl and I struggled to find an appropriate level of contact with these women who had been a vital part of our family. All the family needed to carefully bring our questions out in the open and discuss our feelings about issues:

☐ Are we being disloyal to our own child if we keep in touch with his former spouse? The answer certainly varies from family to family. If there are grandchildren, I feel some contact is very important, particularly if your former in-law child is the parent with major custodial responsibilities.

☐ When, if ever, is it appropriate to invite the former spouse to a family gathering? Our family decided that it depended on the comfort level of the son who had gone through the divorce. Other families might reach different conclusions.

☐ Should we invite a former spouse to special activities that honored the grandchildren? Again, different situations may call for different criteria. Our family felt that the children's wishes should carry some weight in the decision.

Addressing such questions early will make it easier to decide what course of action to take when occasions arise. Tensions may already exist, but talking openly may prevent their escalating. It's much better than allowing misunderstanding to occur and motives to be questioned. The person who has left the family circle may not know where he or she stands now with various members; even if things aren't totally positive, clarifying feelings will allow everyone to operate within reality instead of having to speculate and imagine.

It's Not Easy

This period of redefinition can make us feel afraid, confused, restless, lost. Restlessness is often a precursor to change, though; gradually we will find a sense of direction.

If we have decided that we do want to retain and redefine the relationship with a former in-law child, we will probably have to take the first steps.

Muriel finally wrote to Helene, her former daughter-in-law, after several years of strain and avoidance. She was honest in saying that she felt awkward but wanted to forgive and move to a new beginning—yet didn't know how. She was pleased to receive a positive response; Helene too wanted the tension to be over. These two women became more comfortable seeing each other at the grandson's soccer games because they both knew that the other wanted to let go of the past and work for future harmony.

For many families, a divorce disrupts the traditional and predictable. If there are changes in values and lifestyles, conflicts often arise among family members.

Your suddenly single child may feel empty, like half a person. The separation or divorce leaves a void, and some divorcing individuals have a strong need to quickly fill that vacuum. They are seeking proof that someone can love them regardless of their recent rejection. They begin dating and may bring a new friend to some family activity. Does it catch you off guard? Do you feel pressure to accept this person who is replacing a former spouse? Do you want to say, "I didn't sign up for this; I'm not ready"? The "friend" may have been on the scene before the separation. What are you to think? Should you invest in this friendship? What could it mean for the future? Your ex-in-law could be furious about your acceptance of this "friend." Such tension may seriously complicate the relationship between your child and his or her ex-spouse and add to the difficulty of the divorce for you all. Take your time.

You Can't Please Everyone

Tom and Margery were in shock and found it hard to accept their son's divorce. They hoped that the decision could be reversed. Not enough time had elapsed before they were asked to accept a series of new girlfriends. They disapproved of their son's new, "free" lifestyle, but they did not want to alienate him and end up having no input in his life. It was equally difficult for the siblings in the family to accept that the marriage was over and to welcome their brother's new friends. The grandchildren were confused as well and didn't know how to respond to cousins' questions about their father's new relationships.

Tom and Margery felt embarrassed and caught in the middle. The siblings did not accept their brother's change in values, and he was no longer welcome at family gatherings. To continue supporting their son meant creating separate times to be with him and his girlfriend. The parents were heartsick that the whole family would not be together for their annual holidays.

Our own pattern of frequent family visits back and forth across the state was interrupted by divorce. There weren't the same joy and exuberance at family celebrations and reunions now, because someone we loved was missing. Karl and I experienced real sadness.

Parents can do nothing about the past. But we may have some positive influence on the present and the future if we don't cut off the avenues of communication with our kids. We need the wisdom of Solomon. Biblical standards may have been broken, but we are not our children's judges. We are challenged with what it means to extend grace to them. According to Tim Dearborn, "Grace is therapeutic, redemptive, restorative. Grace is not amnesty—it is not passive on God's part. It cost Him the cross."[1]

With time—years—Karl and I have adjusted to the changes brought about by the decisions our children made. What else could we do? We took small steps, writing cards and letters and arranging short visits here and there. We attempted to offer the kind of love that looks forward instead of backward. By now, some encouraging changes have eased the discomfort.

Emotionally Charged Occasions

As we have already seen, forgiveness and healing come about through growing self-awareness. Sometimes specific events facilitate this awareness and force us to deal with an issue. Of all family celebrations, weddings (whether the remarriage of a child or the marriage of grandchildren) may be the most emotionally charged for families affected by divorce. Former spouses may not be speaking to each other. There may have been little or no personal contact for a long time, and fears of embarrassment and rejection are very real.

If the parents of the bride are divorced and the father is going to give the bride away, where will he sit—next to his former spouse? If he has remarried, where will his new partner sit—should she even be present? What about the two (or more) sets of grandparents: how can they be made comfortable? A large measure of love and patience on the part of everyone involved will help to make this a joyful occasion for the marrying couple.

The wedding hostess at a large West Coast church told of one wedding where the mother of the bride had not seen her former husband for many years. She was still "carrying a torch" and was angry over their divorce. The wedding hostess was sensitive enough to get this woman to verbalize her feelings of insecurity. Being listened to by the hostess affirmed and calmed the mother. And the hostess was able to arrange seating so that tensions were gradually eased through the rehearsal and wedding. The wedding forced a realistic look at the present and facilitated the letting go of the past.

This particular wedding hostess spends considerable time helping each bride and groom identify any points of tension that may exist, so that she can act as an advocate to make their wedding as smooth and tension-free as possible. She also believes that everyone needs to be validated—the divorced father and mother, grandparents, siblings and so on. Being aware that such occasions have potential for hurt as well as joy enables this hostess to be very observant, asking questions and listening so that people are cared for. It's worth the effort to find such a person to work with your family at such an important time.

If there has been an attempt to work through and redefine the character of relationships with former family members *before* events like graduations, weddings, anniversary parties and even funerals occur, much tension and anxiety can be avoided. These special times are fraught with plenty of emotion in and of themselves, without the added ingredient of old, unresolved issues brought about by divorce in the family.

Remarriage: Establishing New Relationships

Great care and sensitive love are needed if and when your children decide to remarry. You may feel that not enough time has elapsed, that more healing needs to take place. You may not feel the new spouse-to-be is as good a match for your son or daughter as the first one was. How will you handle the complex feelings and loyalties? Will you greet this person who plans to join your family with suspicion and indifference, erecting barriers? Will you be able to receive him or her warmly?

Once again, the decision to remarry is made not by you but by your son or daughter, and in Western culture the parents usually have little or no input. So boycotting the marriage or voicing disapproval may accomplish little except to create strained relationships. Your responsibility is to represent the grace and forgiveness of God in the midst of very imperfect circumstances.

You may have strong feelings against the remarriage for a variety of reasons, including biblical ones. It is easier when your children are trying to follow the Lord in their choices. Harold Ivan Smith writes, "If two people have honestly confessed their sins and failures from their first marriage and are willing to commit themselves to a second marriage, the body of Christ ought to affirm them and provide support."[2] Whatever your own situation is, resiliency will be required!

Some parents hesitate to open their hearts to someone new and the possibility of hurt again. Their hesitation may have little to do with who the new partner is, yet the new partner is the one who experiences the distance or disapproval. Then, too, the family shares history that the newcomer is not privy to, and he or she may feel isolation and pain. You may be able (whether you *want* to or not!) to do some filling in, explaining relatives and family memories over a cup of coffee in order to make the new family member feel less of an outsider.

Even in the midst of our lingering pain or discomfort, we parents need to prayerfully and carefully think through the messages that we will communicate. What is this person really like? Can he or she help my child grow, mature and heal? It may be helpful to discuss and clarify your reservations about your child's remarriage with a close friend. You wish to build bridges, not barriers. Pray together for God to prepare your heart to welcome this new family member rather than creating hurt and misunderstanding.

Margery had not completed her grieving over her son's divorce when he decided to remarry. A very close attachment with her former daughter-in-law was still strong, several years after the divorce.

She wasn't ready to give her heart away and went to her new daughter-in-law to try to explain her feelings. She told the new wife not to expect too much from her because she hadn't yet worked through her loss. But her attempt at honesty brought only pain and misunderstanding. The new daughter-in-law felt rejected, and it took a long time to break through the barrier that arose. Our attempts to be honest don't always achieve what we envision. Prayerfully seeing yourself in the other's place may lead you to speak very carefully—or to say nothing.

Several years passed before each of our sons remarried. Slowly each one had experienced healing, working through his pain and failures, getting some counseling, both pastoral and psychological. We now have two new daughters-in-law. I found it helpful to enter into each of these new relationships slowly, getting to know the women who were part of these new beginnings. I needed to be sensitive to the uniqueness of each one and the special gifts that she would bring to the marriage. I tried to put myself in her place and realize where I needed, as future mother-in-law, to be particularly sensitive, aware of possible areas and times of discomfort. I tried to be sensitive to the fact that their weddings shouldn't be compromised because of family history. Even though there were children involved, we wanted to celebrate the new beginnings and welcome these women because our sons loved them.

It's hard not to have family history come up in conversation, so we needed to give them background so they wouldn't feel on the outside looking in. We tried to be honest, not tiptoeing around history but focusing on the present and future with loving acceptance.

It is not always possible to eliminate the names of our former daughters-in-law from the conversation, since they share joint custody of the children. But we realize it is hard for the new wives to be continually reminded of prior marriages. Not everything is smooth all the time, but mutual trust is growing, and Karl and I are genuinely growing in our love for these two women.

Here are some suggestions to consider if your child is getting remarried:

☐ Arrange a time with your child's future spouse for relaxed conversation. Express genuine enthusiasm (if possible) about their plans. Ask if there are things she or he would like to talk about or questions you may be able to answer. Ask questions that will help you know this person better, without probing in areas too personal to be appropriate. Just being heard by each other will be of great value to you both. And you may achieve greater mutual understanding that will make you more comfortable both during the wedding activities and in the future.

☐ Encourage counseling for the new partners—to include their children if it is to be a blended family. This could help them identify possible areas of stress and alert them to possible solutions. Some churches will not perform second marriages without this having taken place. Make it clear that you are not implying they are "sick" or unstable, but that such counsel is useful for every marrying couple in today's complex world.

◻ You may be able to offer financial assistance for counseling. Helping to finance such a step could be an appropriate gift. However, some sons and daughters would view the acceptance of such an offer as a return to dependence and be offended. Consider such an offer carefully.

◻ Recognize that there will be times when you will say or do something you regret. For example, you might without thinking call your new in-law child by the former spouse's name. What to do? Make your apologies and go on. It may be appropriate to talk about it; admit that it may happen again despite your best intentions. A sense of humor helps to ease such situations.

As Harold Ivan Smith puts it, "Remarriage takes time, commitment and patience. But love always pays big dividends."[3]

7

New Roles with Your Grandchildren

•

WHEN ANNETTE'S SON and his wife divorced, some of the joy and light went out in her. Her heart was heavy. She was most concerned for her grandchildren; she longed to reach out to them in their disruption and confusion, but she wasn't sure how.

It was painful to see the grandchildren's fear of abandonment, particularly in the early stages of the separation. Sometimes they seemed to be adjusting well, involved in activities and life as before. Sometimes they withdrew into silence. In those initial weeks of turmoil she felt flashes of anger mixed with sadness as she asked herself, *How can these young, loving parents be so self-centered, disregarding their children's needs and the long-term consequences of their decision?* She had never questioned her son's coping skills, but now she wondered how he would manage as a part-time single parent, with his very full professional life—in the midst of so much pain.

For Karl and me, distance was a handicap to spending time with our grandchildren. We lived six hours' drive from our son Tim's home and had usually seen his family every three or four months. Now the visits were often six or more months apart, and it took longer to fully reconnect with the young ones. They were growing and changing so fast! We weren't as sure of what gifts they would enjoy. How had their interests changed? What was currently important to them? We didn't feel as free and natural as before. We didn't want to pry, and so we found ourselves stiff in conversation. Afterward we would analyze our interactions with them, hoping we had not said or done the wrong thing.

Most of the time spent with our grandchildren was at our family gatherings on holidays or special occasions. These festivities didn't allow much personal visiting with each grandchild, because they wanted to spend time with their cousins. We learned that it was necessary to see the individual families more often. And it was important to plan separate times with each grandchild. We began to make more frequent visits so we could get to the zoo, McDonald's, the bead store and so on. Playing games drew us closer to the children and helped everyone be more at ease.

In between visits, we tried to communicate through postcards and phone calls. But when I am honest, I know my effort was a faltering one. My sense of loss and sorrow created a feeling of inertia. I didn't know, or thought I didn't know, the "right" things to do, so I often failed to do anything.

Looking back, I realize I could have done some things differently. But I know there are years ahead to work at sharing our thoughts and strengthening the bonds of love. There will continue to be awkward times, but I purpose to make a consistent effort to love my grandchildren, for there are still moments of insecurity and difficult adjustments as they fulfill the custody arrangements and live out their daily lives. I am continually challenged to fully trust God with the long-term well-being of these grandchildren who were so deeply affected by divorce.

Long-Term Effects of Divorce

Divorce doesn't stop taking its toll after two years, or when a child turns eighteen, or when the child marries and sets up a new home. Often I have heard adults say things like this:

☐ "There was no dad when I was growing up, so I have trouble relating to men—I have trouble trusting them."

☐ "I've looked for love in all the wrong places, not having strong guidance from an involved father."

☐ "Mom was so busy trying to survive that she had little time for us. She was always tired."

☐ "There was little joy at home. I left as soon as I possibly could."

This long-term impact shows up in sociological research. Judith Wallerstein's *Second Chances* presents findings about previously unrealized long-term effects on the children of divorce. She and her associates were the first researchers to follow families and children for at least ten and in some cases fifteen years. A sample of her observations is, "The Moores' divorce produced in Denise deep-seated anxieties about relationships, fears that she banished to the farthest recesses of her mind. But the feelings endured, only to resurface years later."[1]

Wallerstein considered this a "sleeper effect" of divorce. She says, "The sleeper effect is particularly dangerous because it occurs at a crucial time when many young women make decisions that have long-term implications in their lives. Entering young adulthood, they are faced with issues of commitment, love, and sex in an adult context—and they are aware that the game is serious.

"If they tie in with the wrong man, have children too soon or choose harmful lifestyles, the effect can be long-lasting and tragic. Suddenly overcome by fears and anxieties, they begin to make connections between these feelings and their parents' divorce."[2]

Wallerstein was often asked by children of divorce, "How can you believe in commitment when anyone can change their mind at any time?" She responds: "A significant number of young women are living with an intolerable level of anxiety about betrayal."[3] Because, following divorce, the girls were usually well-adjusted during adolescence and through high school, the troubles experienced at entry into young adulthood came as a complete surprise.

Clearly the fear of abandonment lingers a long time. When divorced parents move on to establish new relationships, the children may feel disregarded and set aside. Many divorcing adults have very limited understanding of the long-term ripple effects of their decisions to divorce, and they may enter into remarriage or new relationships much too quickly. When they do, it means more adjustments and possible emotional overload for their children. It is not uncommon in our current cultural climate for several temporary relationships to occur before a permanent partnership in committed marriage is established. The children of divorce may find it hard to let another person into their hearts because "you'll just leave me like the rest."

How Do I Fit In?

I hear you saying, "What does all this have to do with me? What has happened has happened; I can't change it." True, you can't change it—but you can *be there* for the grandchildren.

We grandparents need to realize how important our contribution may be to the long-term well-being of the family. It's hard for children to rebuild trust after being hurt. What they need is consistent sensitivity and love. That's what you can give. Keep in mind that during times of turmoil and change the children's relationship with Grandma and Grandpa may be the most stable, accepting, dependable one in their lives.

If you live near your grandchildren, you can make a significant contribution through your involvement in routine activities, where they can observe your values lived out. Some of these "routine" events will later be recalled as favorite childhood memories. Your loving presence demonstrates continuity, helpfulness and patience—qualities children need to internalize. Seeing that you can rise above the difficulty encourages them to believe they can too. Even though it's difficult to do, trust can be rebuilt.

A couple of our friends have made a determined effort to stay connected to their grandson and former daughter-in-law since their son's divorce. They live in the same community. The boy was in grammar school when his parents divorced. The grandparents maintained ongoing contact by offering him meals and overnight visits, and they included him in recreational activities and an occasional trip. That gave his mom some free time, as well. They have also kept in touch with their former daughter-in-law through phone calls and visits. Even though they've not always agreed with her decisions, they have tried to be supportive of her as a person of worth. The boy's dad, now living in a different part of the country, appreciated his parents' involvement with his son.

Recently these friends hosted their grandson and a few of his friends, his mother, maternal grandmother and great-grandmother, for his eighteenth-birthday celebration. They had a wonderful time! This couple did not hang on to their initial despair and anger. Prayerfully they came to a place of forgiveness. "Without forgiveness," my friend said, "we could not have kept a vital relationship." Not long ago we were present at the grandparents' fiftieth-wedding-anniversary dinner, where this young man told everyone present how much his grandparents' love and support had meant to him over the years.

These grandparents provided an anchor—a place where he was always welcome, where he could receive love and perspective and a sense of continuity. This young man also benefited from an active Christian faith which his grandparents modeled for him over the years.

Not all of us will do as well as this couple, but we can try. And we will have much more opportunity to build a strong long-term relationship with our grandchildren if we make an effort to maintain communication with their parents.

With the breakup of a marriage, your child and in-law child will be unusually vulnerable to pain. Any words of disapproval or any advice that seems like criticism will assault their bruised self-esteem and do more harm than good. And comments you make to or around grandchildren will likely go back to their parents and intensify any tensions you already have with them. Any implied judgment on how they are handling things, no matter how justified it may be, will only make the relationship more difficult. So keep in mind that your words to your grandchildren should always be helpful ones that add stability to their churning world.

There may be times of strain between you and your grandchild. There may be silence, or you may sense a desire on the child's part to remain detached. That hurts. You can state your desire to talk about the circumstances and feelings but also your willingness to respect their need *not* to talk. If the time comes when they are ready to open up, they may then come to you.

Passing Along Good Values
When the communication and the relationships are good

between the older and younger generations, the older ones can hope to provide useful input and feedback. I was privileged recently to have a conversation with Robert Aldrich, retired pediatric physician teaching at the University of Washington Medical School. He had this to say: "Grandparents have a different value system than young people today, and grandparenting gives them the opportunity to transmit those values to a new generation. They could be a major force in this country."

He added, "You can't turn society's problems around by introducing new laws; you have to introduce a change in cultural values and attitudes. There's where grandparents come in. Demonstrate your values about respect, honesty, responsibility and so on in positive and consistent ways, exposing your grandchildren to time-honored principles that have worked for you."

We are tempted to worry and meddle. We may observe our children vying for favored-parent status and giving inconsistent or insufficient discipline. The noncustodial parent who has little time with his or her children may create a "party time" or "Disneyland" atmosphere. Sometimes parents compete at giving extravagant gifts to gain favor. As grandparents, we should try to be fair and consistent and avoid getting caught in these same patterns.

When children are living with just one parent, some grandparents worry that the young children are forced to accept more responsibility and give more household help than they should have to. However, it is necessary and even valuable for them to contribute to family life at an appropriate level. They can gain a sense of belonging and pride from the skills that they learn. My grandson loved to share the cookies he had baked and show us the hay he'd moved into the barn. We could genuinely affirm him—and that helped him move toward maturity.

Let your contribution be one of praising and building up your grandchild. Don't spend your energy worrying about the things you cannot change. Grandparents can hold on to the thought that God, in his love, will aid and strengthen them and trust that balance and harmony will be achieved, while not expecting it to happen overnight.

Don't Ask Too Many Questions

Use discretion when asking such questions as, "What is happening at home?" "What is your mom [dad] doing?" "What did you do this weekend?" It can make the child uncomfortable. And your questions may be passed on to the parents, causing them to feel, if they are already somewhat defensive, that you are prying into their private business via the kids. Questions that would have been very natural before the divorce are not appropriate now. You may feel isolated and hurt because your motives and genuine interest are now suspect.

Try to be patient. Your ongoing visiting and contact may be at stake. With care you can keep conversation light: tell about some of your own activities and express your interest in positive ways. Ask questions such as: "What have you done lately that was fun?" "I hear you got an A on your science project. What was your experiment?" It's hard work to keep your balance when walking on eggshells, but it is worth it, isn't it?

Custody Concerns

Custody arrangements may be a source of concern. I know one grandmother who was deeply troubled because her grandchildren were exposed to a homosexual household when they visited their noncustodial parent. How would this nontraditional partnership affect the grandchildren? Others worry when the children visit parents' homes that seem unsafe due to alcohol, a violent temper, overpermissiveness or other problems. I don't have any simple answers here. I encourage you to surround these children with your prayers for guidance, protection and wisdom. (The next two chapters will take up some of these issues more fully.)

One mother, caught in such a dilemma, was able to explain to her children that their father had gone through some serious changes in his life. Because of these changes she planned very short visiting periods, easing the grandparents' concerns as well as her own.

Custody arrangements cause deep concern for the parents themselves, of course. There is usually a desire to disrupt the children's lives as little as possible while meeting each parent's need. But there may also be an attempt to get back at or make life difficult for the other spouse, regardless of the consequences for the children.

According to an article by Clare Ansberry, "In recent years psychologists and child custody specialists have generally agreed that joint and more flexible sole custody agreements should help children by assuring them that they haven't lost either parent. When the parents are in the same community, joint custody is less disruptive to the child than when there is considerable travel time between the two homes. An increasing number of children are becoming regular commuters."[4]

"Sometimes things work better on paper than in real life," others have commented. Others observe that joint custody is unsettling. Children need *one* place to call home.

Some children are quoted in the article as saying, "Sometimes I don't know where I'm going—I'm confused about whose house I'm supposed to be at." Or, "Shuttling back and forth, I don't really feel like I have a home." As the grandparents stand in the wings and observe, it is both a challenge and an opportunity to continue to be an ongoing, predictable, loving presence in the grandchild's life.

Parents who divorce may fail to notice that they are changing one of their own parents' most treasured relationships—their relationship to their grandchildren. Your children may not intend to cause you pain any more than they want to cause their own children pain. But the pain is there.

Sometimes, when there has been little or no resolution of the conflict between the divorcing parents, grandparents are denied access to grandchildren. That brings pain and a sense of isolation. Grandparent advocacy groups in some areas are seeking to bring about legislation to protect the rights of visitation for grandparents. You may wish to be a part of such a group if this is your concern.

Even when you are not denied access, it is hard to keep a close bond with grandchildren when distance limits your visits. To compensate, one grandmother I know reads books into a tape recorder to her young grandchildren, then sends both the tape and the books to them. Another grandfather, who loved to make up stories, used to do the same and send the cassettes in hand-decorated packages, allowing the child to catch his message of love and caring as well as the story. Now that his grandfather has died, I'm sure those taped stories are a precious keepsake for this young man. Such gifts say, "You are special to me and I value you enough to spend time with you even though we can't be together in the same place."

Robert Aldrich makes these suggestions:

☐ Be confident that your time and attention can make a difference, even if it is not evident at present.

☐ Be available to attend sports events, school programs and teacher conferences that parents can't attend. This helps the child to feel important and supported.

☐ Let the child know that he or she can come to your house if you live close by. It helps break patterns of loneliness and allows you to listen to the child's feelings and concerns.

☐ Having the grandchild at your house gives you time to do

some activities with just him or her, to help develop pride in accomplishment and to teach some specific skills.

☐ Give each grandchild a special place for their things (even if it's only a drawer)—a place that remains constant, where their treasures won't be disturbed.

☐ If the visit is longer, establish a routine so children will know what to expect.

☐ Encourage them to ask questions; listen to their concerns and clarify what may be confusing to them if you are able.

☐ Do your best to make it clear to the grandchildren that their parents' breakup is not their fault and that there is nothing that they can do to put it back together. Give information, but avoid blaming.

☐ When mothers are left with the larger share of custody and often a reduced income, grandparents may provide help through special gifts of equipment and school funds as well as the usual birthday and holiday gifts.

☐ Offer to babysit so that the custodial parent has time away from parenting responsibilities.

☐ Offer to help with family chores. Even a half-day a week might ease your daughter or son's load and provide a natural time with the grandchildren. [I remember many wonderful times sitting near my grandmother while she folded clothes or baked. It gave us a time to talk. I sometimes read to her while she worked, and sometimes I could help.]

☐ "By the time you are a grandparent you have learned many things: greater patience, acceptance of life as a dynamic, ever-changing state, as well as skills that make you a valuable person for your grandchild to know."

☐ "You may have overcome serious adversity; this, too, can be a positive contribution to your family."[5]

These suggestions may seem obvious to you who are grandparents, but when we are hurt and confused, we may overlook the obvious—I did. I'm certain that many of you have found a variety of other ways to support and love your children and grandchildren through their crisis. It's an investment that takes a lot of energy and time, and one from which you may not see immediate fruit. But you can know that, over the long haul, *your input is important and you do make a difference.*

8

When Your Child Is an Unfit Parent

•

I HAD DRIVEN, ON A cold February afternoon, to a rural community at the base of Mount Rainier to meet Sydney, the founder of a support group for grandparents who were rearing grandchildren. A young, attractive grandmother greeted me warmly and seated me at the table in her cheery kitchen.

As we talked about the circumstances that led to forming this group, I began to see in her a clear demonstration of what I have been saying throughout this book. Through her some-times painful growing self-awareness, she had discovered that there were choices to be made. She had courageously sought to live out Christian values in the face of most difficult circumstances resulting from a son's divorce, and she had been willing to risk involvement. I report Sydney's story here to show the process each of us goes through, even though the exact circumstances and consequences of our choices may be vastly different.

Sydney's Story

With a small sigh, Sydney began:

"My son sees his little daughter here in my home at times that I determine, to maintain her best interests and safety. I have pretty much let go of the fact that neither he nor his former wife wants to be more involved in her life, even though that fact is a source of tremendous hurt for me. My husband and I pretty much live each day doing what we need to do, and I pray a lot.

"Terry was a 'casual' drug user in his teens. Many times I had rescued him in an attempt to straighten him out. Wasn't that what I was supposed to do? I had been raised in the church and trained to accept my responsibilities. I didn't have a clue that I wasn't helping him."

After Terry went into the service and returned to some drug use, Sydney continued to rescue. When he was AWOL, she found him and took him back to his military base so his penalty would be less severe. "Wasn't that my Christian responsibility?" she asked rhetorically. "I kept thinking it was."

In his early twenties, he and his girlfriend decided to marry. "It was a rather abrupt decision, but I thought, well, maybe this will be good for them, settle them down a bit. It never occurred to me that Mary Ann might be pregnant!" she said with indignation.

Terry was gone when his young wife went into labor. Sydney, a first-time grandmother, was there to fill the gap and be the birthing coach. She had always wanted a girl, and now she was the first to hold her precious granddaughter. She was delighted to bond with this baby girl. When the mother seemed disinterested, not wanting even to hold the baby, Sydney was puzzled. Her son didn't appear for several days. "I didn't raise him like this. I felt that he was missing something he would never, ever recover."

When Terry did come, his first question was, "What does she look like?" Sydney, with pride, told him, "She looks just like you, the same birthmarks and everything. She's the image of you!" He began to sob and mumbled, "Well, I didn't even know for sure if she was mine."

Unable to Be Good Parents

Several weeks later, Terry came to her saying he didn't like the way Mary Ann was caring for the baby. "It really frightens me! She hangs over the crib and screams at the baby, 'Shut up, shut up!' She's shaking her too!"

Sydney's face reflected the pain of these past events as she told me, "It was now very apparent that drugs were back in the picture."

She felt compelled to get involved. With the father's full cooperation, Child Protective Services placed the baby with Sydney and her husband under a "temporary shelter care" provision. She felt relieved that Anna was safe in her care, but angry, too, because the parents seemed unable to accept responsibility for their child. During the months that followed, her son obtained a divorce and custody of the baby.

Sydney's feelings about the divorce were overshadowed by her agony as the courts sent Anna to her maternal grandmother, who had shown little interest. Sydney felt the decision was unfair to the child, and—now cut off from visits—she missed the baby terribly. In time, however, through the efforts of lawyers, it was shown that Sydney was the one who had demonstrated the necessary stability and interest, and Anna was returned to Sydney for permanent care and custody. With quiet, deep emotion Sydney shared, "From the things that I have since learned, I believe that what Anna's parents did in giving up their daughter was an act of love."

Sometime after Anna's birth, Sydney began to realize that she herself needed help. "I began going back to church. I believe that God had a plan and I needed to get my eyes open and see what was really going on."

Learning New Patterns

She began going to Al-Anon, an Alcoholics Anonymous affiliate for people affected by a family member's substance abuse. "There, I got my first real glimmer that the things I had done to rescue Terry hadn't helped him. I hadn't meant to be part of the problem by repeatedly rescuing him, but I had been doing that. I learned that a drug is a drug, whether it is alcohol or an illegal substance such as cocaine, crack or whatever. I got some real insight into myself and into what was going on with him. That led me into counseling and into a Christian support group for codependents and people who had come out of dysfunctional families."

Her voice dropped as she acknowledged, "I had gone to the group for two months before I ever spoke. I would stand in a circle as others prayed and tears would fill my eyes. I couldn't speak, because part of me had put up a wall to take care of myself, not knowing what else to do. In getting healthy myself, I've had to let that wall down, even though I recognize that at times some of it still exists."

About the same time that Sydney decided to stop taking responsibility for her son's choices and commit him to God, her son made the decision to return to drug and alcohol dependency treatment. Sydney rejoiced—she thought that after the drug treatment program was over, her son would take a more active part in his daughter's life. It didn't happen. According to the experts, drug use had interrupted his maturation. He had lost his prime teen years, and now he had to catch up. He wasn't ready to be a father.

Sydney feels moments of resentment that her son isn't the

one dealing with his daughter's care. "It's really scary," she said, "when I begin to get inklings of future abnormal behavior in my granddaughter—the kind I see in other drug-affected children. It was also scary to face that future without additional support, so I advertised in the newspaper for response from other grandparents who might be rearing their grandbabies. I thought perhaps we could learn from each other."

Now a core group of approximately fifteen meets weekly, joined by about that many more who come part of the time. They call themselves the OWLS (Oldies With Little Ones). "A few of us are Christians, but that isn't the focus. We don't want to keep people away because of past negative impressions of church or Christianity. Some may see a difference in the way we cope with things and they may ask about it; that's fine."

Some of the group members have grandchildren who have been sexually molested, emotionally abused, neglected or abandoned. Most of the parents of these children were chemically dependent. "These grandparents are appalled to have reared children who have turned out like this," she said. She was quick to point out that "most of us are regular people with a solid work ethic and a basic set of values. We have other children who are fine. My son was adopted; now that I have inquired, I've learned that his biological parents and grandparents were alcoholics, leaving this boy predisposed to addiction."

People often ask what it's like to parent the second time around. Sydney and other OWLS point out that their inconvenience is secondary. "We do the same things that we did the first time. I don't have as much energy, but I do have more patience and a more realistic perspective about what is important. I'm not as concerned about what other people think, and I do what I feel is important for this child."

There was a vibrancy in Sydney's voice as she told about the answers she sought for her granddaughter and what she was learning from research going on locally and in a large teaching hospital nearby: "Anna is a drug-affected child, and I am dealing with what is called 'heightened behavior' or the 'drug effect.' It is an increased sensitivity to change and to sounds and an inability to connect an event or behavior with the consequence. Children in this category are often destructive and cruel to pets. Some are already self-destructive at two years of age. In a noisy, unfocused group they go to pieces. I may find it hard to place her in day care later on, if she develops these behaviors. I have also learned that by school age such behavior frequently turns outward.

"At times it's hard to believe what the research is showing. The OWLS group is helpful and understanding even when I choose denial as a means of coping. As a fellow struggler I have learned that there is a physiological reason for Anna's difficult behaviors, that she isn't just being naughty, stubborn or defiant. It doesn't solve the problems I face, but it helps explain it. It moderates some of the guilt feelings."

Sydney's Choices: What Did They Bring?

As I drove home that day, I couldn't help but admire this woman's courage in the face of such a challenge. Sydney's story is far more dramatic than mine, and perhaps more than yours as well. Each one of us experiences our own set of circumstances, but those circumstances evoke similar emotions and responses: The broken expectations for our children cause us pain. Our pride is hurt. We feel both sad and angry over the circumstances that culminate in divorce. The choices that have been made may result in feelings of personal grief. And we worry about the outcome as we look into the future.

As Sydney processed these emotions, there came a point when she had to accept the realities: her son was divorced and there was no safe place for her granddaughter. Her focus had to shift to the child. She faced a huge choice: would she get more deeply involved?

We all need to be able to forgive what we interpret to be mistakes, our own as well as others', and begin to look at how to become a part of the healing process. This was what Sydney tried to do. It meant reaching out for help: to God, to the professional community, to her church and her peers for support. Through her return to the church she got involved with Christian counseling and a group that supported her learning process.

Redefining her relationships meant forgiving her son and letting go; it meant seeing her son's giving up of his child as an act of loving protection for the child. Would she choose to act as mother now, as well as grandmother? What would it mean in the present? What would it cost in the future?

Sydney's hopes for her son's greater involvement in his daughter's life are not yet a reality. Perhaps the future will bring about those longed-for changes. In the meantime, Sydney's grandmothering brings everyday challenges. She has chosen to live with the scary reality of drug-affected behavior and has courageously gathered support to meet her challenges through her church and the establishment of OWLS. She has committed herself to little Anna and has become an advocate for others in similar situations.

I believe that God is bringing good out of a very difficult circumstance that was committed to him by a woman who, at great personal sacrifice and financial cost, was willing to risk long-term involvement. Her story is an encouragement to the rest of us.

9

Facing Embarrassing and Shameful Truths

●

PATRICIA AND JOHN had barely absorbed the shock of their daughter's separation from her husband when they learned the shocking truth behind the breakup: their son-in-law was a homosexual. This quiet couple felt ill-prepared to cope with the truth that shattered their daughter's life and their own.

Sexual abuse, drug or alcohol abuse, live-in lovers and homosexuality were topics seldom discussed or even acknowledged a decade or two ago. Now they are thrust on us on the six o'clock news, on talk shows, in mainstream magazines, in newspapers—and sometimes in our own families. When these issues hit home, many of us are wracked by fear, angry disapproval, resentment and confusion. We don't know what to say or how to act.

In our confusion and concern, we often retreat to an

unhealthy silence. Already drained by their own battles, our sons or daughters may lack the courage to ask what is behind the tension or distance they sense in us. The walls go up and the masks stay on. We need to work hard to figure out our own feelings and what is behind them.

Anne had to work through her fear of speaking out. "I felt real anguish about my daughter's live-in relationship following her divorce. I had shrunk from the risk of rejection, but I knew that I needed to say what was in my heart."

Eventually Anne gained the courage to talk about her concerns with this daughter. Wasn't she compromising her long-held Christian values? What kind of moral statement did this make to her young son? There were many questions. When she finally did speak her mind, she felt free. She realized that her resentment and disapproval had built up because she had been unwilling to verbalize her expectations and concern. Now she wasn't asking her daughter to read her thoughts or figure out why she was strained around her.

Anne communicated clearly, even through some tears. Feelings were out in the open. Whether her daughter's behavior changed or not was the daughter's responsibility; at least Anne had been honest and had taken responsibility for her feelings. She no longer harbored hidden resentment. Conveying those negative feelings as honestly and lovingly as she knew how kept her from building a wall between herself and her adult daughter.

Abuse

Family abuse is one of the hardest circumstances we can face. When it appears, we parents must seek self-awareness, take responsibility for our feelings, communicate honestly and determine limits for personal involvement in our children's lives. When one learns about or observes physical or verbal (rage) abuse, substance (alcohol or drug) abuse, or acts of sexual abuse, it means others in the family circle also are being affected and there is great potential for harm. Fears arise—fears that the situation won't change and that the long-term effect will be devastating.

You may not have learned that abuse was a factor in your child's marriage until after the separation or even the divorce. (Several respondents to my survey told how difficult it had been to help their parents understand that abuse, in some form, had contributed to the breakup.) The way you responded to this knowledge depended on whether your child was being abused, your child was the abuser or your grandchildren were the object of abuse.

A pastor and his wife tell this story: The daughter of a friend of theirs was divorced, and the entire religious community condemned her. She bore the condemnation in silence and moved out of town. Years later, it was learned that she had been the victim of severe physical abuse. Out of consideration for her children, she did not want her husband's sins to become the talk of the town. So she took his guilt on her own shoulders.

Parents must be aware that they probably don't know the whole story. Their child may be much more saintly—or much more of a sinner—than they suspect.

Recognition of abuse may force some emotionally painful realizations on parents. Debra Pearce, a therapist who focuses her family therapy practice in this area, believes "abuse seldom starts without some history in previous generations. It reflects forces in the family system. If I were a parent and saw abusive behavior in my child's marriage, I might tend to overlook it or distance myself if I had not resolved related issues in my own history or marriage.

"We tend to go as far with others in their pain as we've gone in our own pain," Pearce continues. "Once they can look at their own issues, parents are more willing to acknowledge what's going on in their children's situation. If you do acknowledge what's happening, you must address the issue of boundaries of their privacy. At what point would your responsive actions become intrusive? What are some possible consequences? You may need to consider when to let go and say, 'Okay, that's their life. They've made their decisions and they are responsible for them.' "[1]

What Part Should I Play?

How can we, as parents and grandparents, express our concern in loving and nonthreatening ways, even though it may not be heeded?

Some authorities say, "Don't give advice if you are not asked for it." Even therapists hesitate to give much advice. They listen a lot and ask penetrating questions. Questioning is the mildest form of confrontation and can be very helpful.

Pearce suggests, "You could offer a *safe harbor* for your child and/or grandchildren in times of need. Living arrangements may be in flux during separation or divorce. Occasionally there's a need for safety from an abusive, live-in partner following divorce or when there has been a remarriage.

"If you do intervene and offer a *safe place,* you need to express your expectations and set limits for its duration: who pays the bills, what the house rules will be, etc. Your desire is to be helpful, not to encourage or enable weakness or recurrences of the abuse. Initially, it may be hard to have a clear idea what those limits should be. This could be especially true if the adult child has not fully individuated [become his or her own person apart from the parents and family]. It may be necessary and very wise to seek professional counsel at this point."[2]

If your adult child moves home to escape an abusive spouse, you may be endangered too. A court injunction, restricting the abusive spouse's access to the family, is an option but isn't always foolproof. You may be able to help by doing some research about what resources are available locally. A shelter for battered women, which many communities offer, may be a better choice than your home. Such shelters provide confidential, temporary, safe refuge for both women and children. Many also provide counseling along with help in locating housing, child care and short-term financial assistance. Prayerfully seek to find the balance that is most helpful—that allows your child to grow toward full individuation into adulthood and does not encourage dependence on you.

In a metropolitan area there may be a variety of public agencies and programs to assist the family. Many communities have crisis phone hotlines that can offer perspective in an emergency. Some children's hospitals assign parent aides to families caught in abusive patterns, helping to teach anger management and better parenting skills.

When Violence Threatens

You may need to shift from restraint to intervention if you observe harsh things happening to your grandchildren. You may become aware they're being hurt and cannot protect themselves. Pearce advises "calling the parents' attention to what you see going on. If one or both parents are the abuser, Child Protective Services is an alternative. Someone has to be an advocate for the children."[3] Without help and support these children will become adults who struggle with low self-esteem and have difficulty trusting in relationships.

"Don't be surprised, however," Pearce adds, "if the kids get angry with you. They may be thinking, 'They're trying to take me away from my parents!' Later on they might see that somebody did care what was happening. It can be very helpful to have a neutral, experienced person coordinate the intervention. There is no guarantee that your intervention will make a difference, but at least it serves notice that someone cares."[4]

In *Shame-Free Parenting,* Sandra D. Wilson helps parents identify unhealthy parenting patterns and develop healthy ones so their children can grow up free of shame. While it is specifically addressed to parents, the book can help to educate grandparents as well. It includes a list of "indicators of sexual abuse."[5] These indicators are given for various age groups and might prove very helpful to clarify what you may have observed or what to look for if you suspect sexual abuse.

Fears and uncertainties about the consequences of intervention have to be examined. Seek professional counsel. Pastor Tim Snow says, "Hopefully family relationships are strong enough to endure confrontation. The basis of a healthy relationship is not agreement on everything, but being able to encounter and love each other in hard ways."[6]

Some grandparents may ask, "If I say something, will I be refused contact with my grandchild? Will my child cut off relationship with me?" That is always the risk when you confront. But is the fear of rejection or loss of relationship so great that you can ignore or deny the probability of real danger?

If you strongly believe your grandchildren are in danger and you have checked for other resources and gotten no help, you can contact your state's department of children's protective services. It is primarily concerned with keeping families together, but it has the power to remove children from the home when that is necessary. It represents the authority of the state and sends a powerful message to the abuser and/or sick family system. Be aware that *you may be setting powerful wheels in motion, particularly with respect to sexual abuse.* If you are unsure, it would be wise to first inquire, anonymously, about the policies and services in your area, to find out what you can expect. Call your local community service or human resources department, your local library or the nonemergency number at the police department.

Lifestyle Changes

Parents seldom have a full understanding of the reasons for their children's divorce. John and Patricia were understandably stunned when they learned that their son-in-law was leaving the marriage to take a male partner. They had developed a loving parental relationship with this young man, and they grieved not only for the dissolution of a decade of marriage but also for the other choices he was making. The whole family agonized over bitterly contested custody and visitation rights. The daughter had known about her husband's gay lifestyle but had hoped things could change. When they didn't, she felt not only anger and loss but also shame.

Patricia says, "Our daughter was a victim. Her husband was always gay, but we had no idea." It took a long time to work through the feelings of betrayal, abandonment and shame. She adds, "If someone hasn't walked where you are walking, it's very difficult for them to give you any support. We felt so alone. People can befriend you and pray for you, but it's not the same as life experience."

Another couple, Hazel and Wayne, also felt betrayal and shame when their daughter-in-law left their son, declaring herself a lesbian. They had enjoyed a very loving relationship with the young woman, and her new lifestyle choice (which they believed to be wrong in the sight of God) was very hard for them to understand or accept. Hazel confided, "I cried for days and searched the Scriptures for help. I journaled like crazy, writing out my grief and anger. I've lost several family members in death, but I really believe that this is worse. At times I want to strike back, even though a part of me doesn't want to."

Wayne's quiet response to his pain was more typical of fathers I have talked with: "There is nothing I can do, so we must just go on." Because there were no grandchildren from this marriage, it was a little easier to put the whole thing to rest and move on.

Both these couples have a vital Christian faith and had reared their children as believers. Prayer—their own and that of others—was a vital resource.

Living Together Outside of Marriage

Many parent couples have told me how hard it was to cope with a divorced child's decision to enter into a living arrangement outside of marriage. Your child's decision may have been arrived at with much soul-searching. Having gone through a divorce, he or she now has questions about long-term commitment in marriage a second time: *Will I fail again?* Need for companionship as well as economic advantage is cited as a logical reason for living together. Not everyone agonizes over such a choice, but if you do, I understand your pain.

Pastor and author Bruce Larson notes, "The national ethic used to be that you didn't have sexual intimacy outside of marriage. It did happen, of course, but it was considered wrong by the vast majority of our society and almost all the Christian community. Today, society is saying it is okay. But as Christians we need to remind our children that our allegiance is to Jesus Christ, and He had a lot to say about lifestyles."[7] Gerhard Hauer has a good section called "Christians, Tenderness and Sexuality" in his book *Longing for Tenderness.*[8]

Some parents withdraw from sons and daughters who are cohabiting, unwilling to invest emotionally in a temporary relationship. Others feel sorrow, both because their own values have been rejected and because they know what pain may result. Now that the threat of sexual disease is very real, parents also fear for their children's health. Parents feel confused. The familiar expectations and ways of relating don't always apply. There is uncertainty about what to say and how to say it. If you speak your mind you may alienate yourself from your child, especially if you do it in an unloving way.

Parents grope for ways to adjust. They ask: "How should I introduce my child's partner—as his friend? Do I invite the partner for family holidays? How emotionally involved should I get?" Will the relationship lead to marriage? If it does and you have not accepted this person, will you find yourself not invited to the wedding? What if you are invited but don't feel you can go? Any hostility that builds up will be very hard to resolve. One parent said, "I'm damned if I do and damned if I don't."

Many wonder how to handle the sleeping arrangement for overnight visits from a child and his or her partner. If you experience tension here, you are a part of a large company. Columnist Abigail Van Buren ("Dear Abby") regularly tells readers: "It is your home and you have the privilege of telling guests where they will sleep. Simply say, 'Jane, you may have the guest room and John will sleep in the small bedroom upstairs.' " Of course, your child may choose to stay in a hotel or not come to visit at all.

Russell and Betty did a lot of soul-searching about the overnight use of their retreat condo by some of their children and their partners. Betty felt deep convictions about keeping their retreat unviolated. She realized that "my refusal might not keep the children out of bed, but they didn't need to do it in my space or with my consent." Once the parents had established this policy, they could relax and let go of the issue.

It is natural to be uneasy about making your convictions known when your child is disregarding your values. But sometimes you are blessed with an opening. When Jeannette's son's girlfriend asked to talk, Jeannette shared her Christian conviction that intimacy outside of marriage was wrong and what the young people were experiencing was counterfeit joy and an incomplete relationship. She urged Beth to return to her long-abandoned Christian values. This conversation became a turning point for Beth, one which led to her seeking

107

forgiveness and a return to God. This couple terminated their relationship, and several years later Beth married and was able to experience true joy.

The Fellowship of Suffering

We need to be reminded that we are not responsible for our adult child's choices, nor is our identity or value determined by their decisions. These truths are harder to accept when parents haven't let their child really become an adult prior to the crisis. Nevertheless, we are called to love. Sometimes that means risking involvement beyond our comfort zone. Sometimes it calls us to remain silent. Sometimes love means letting go.

In his counseling with parents, Bruce Larson often shares Philippians 3:8-10, in which Paul talks about knowing Christ, the power of his resurrection and the fellowship of his suffering. What is the fellowship of his suffering, and why did Paul think it important? Larson says, "It isn't having cancer, getting old and having Alzheimer's disease—we certainly don't choose these. The fellowship of suffering is to love people as Christ did and still watch them walk away and do the wrong thing. God loves everybody, but He doesn't make them love Him back, nor does He make them do the moral thing. God will not change people unless they allow Him to do so."[9]

Larson goes on to apply this to parents whose children divorce. "When you go through something like divorce with the people you love the most, you hear them say, 'I've got to do my thing.' Still you continue to love them. That, to me, is the fellowship of suffering. It breaks our hearts as surely as it breaks the heart of God. We can avoid the heartbreak by washing our hands of the whole thing, writing our children off and saying, 'It's not my problem, you're wrong and I don't need that kind of pain.' Or, we can accept the realization that, while we are powerless to make them change, we continue to demonstrate our love for them while experiencing a broken heart."[10]

We can pray, "Lord, what do you want to teach me, and what does it mean to love in these painful circumstances in which I find myself?" Then we can listen for God's answer and pray for strength to follow through.

10

Fathers Speak
Out About Their
Children's Divorces

●

THIS BOOK HAS BEEN written primarily from a woman's perspective, but divorce is a family matter. I want to give the fathers a chance to tell their own stories. Their personal struggles, concerns and solutions are woven into every chapter. But their direct accounts may give husbands and wives added insight into how the other's gender, personality and family of origin color their response to divorcing offspring.

* * *

John

John had to adjust to long-term involvement with three generations when his daughter moved back home, bringing her kids with her.

The hardest thing to see in my lifetime was the moving van pulling into our driveway with all Miriam's belongings. Eleven years of my daughter's marriage in the driveway in a truck. This was it! We put it into our basement—eleven years' worth. It really hit home to me. The end had come and here was the accumulation—just things. Finality. There was nothing left as far as the marriage was concerned.

Now, with two young children and their mother, we had three generations in our household. It was a continuing challenge to find balance between parenting once again and taking things as they came. Forty years ago, when young people returned to the nest they would expect to conform to parents' wishes. Not now! They say, "I'm my own person." Maybe that's better, I don't know, but it was sometimes hard to take.

*   *   *

Karl

Karl struggled with the loss of two daughters-in-law he deeply loved, and he worried about his grandchildren's future.

Because several years have passed, the early details of our son's divorces have slipped away now. But it was a terrible shock that these women whom we loved as daughters-in-law were no longer to be in the family. It took a while to realize what a fracture that would produce. For a while it was like a total cutoff, as if *we* were divorced along with our boys.

I felt some rejection and confusion, wondering, "How could you come to this decision?" I felt so helpless. I reasoned that healing could take place between them if they really worked at it. Each one had made decisions that weren't corrected early enough in their marriages, and to them these differences seemed irreconcilable.

When this all started, Elaine spent some sleepless nights and went through a lot of anguish. I don't remember sleeplessness, but I was certainly sad. The loss, you know—how can you help it?

Some folks say it's like a death in the family; yes, death

without a burial. A heaviness that you carry around—a heavy, helpless feeling. There is no termination. It just goes on and on.

My greatest hurt was seeing how the grandchildren have been affected, some more than others. I occasionally feel some awkwardness when we are together, but part of that I guess is just a common response of teenagers to my generation. I'd like to bridge that gap and regain a freedom like we had with them as young children.

As a grandparent it is always a challenge not to participate in the competition of gift-giving. We have ten grandchildren. Our resources are limited and must be spread out. Not every grandparent is in this position; some have more freedom to be involved in satisfying the children's desires.

I know that it is important to be able to talk about pain, to help release it. I was a part of a small group and did share my feelings and our situation. You feel, though, that you don't want to be careless with private family matters. I don't know why I feel that way; it's sort of protective, I guess. Our other two children, whose families are intact, were a wonderful support, but sometimes I think they wondered at the intensity of our emotions.

I realized that it was important to have some escape, something physical to do. I go fishing once in a while, and that gives me an opportunity to forget for a time. I also try to walk regularly. Sometimes Elaine and I find that walking together is a good time to talk. She may feel things more intensely than I do, but it's been hard for both of us. It's sort of irreparable, so you have to pick up and love the new mates that your children have chosen. It's different, though—our former daughters-in-law are still the mothers of our grandchildren.

Hardship can draw couples together or drive a wedge between them. We were drawn together. These were our children, and we needed to support them together. Prayer has been our greatest asset. I believe our reliance on God's faithfulness, his mercy and love for our children, even when they failed one another, was our foundation.

Looking back, I don't think we would have done things much differently. We tried, the best way we knew how, to continue to be loving and supportive. I sometimes wondered what we did when they were growing up that set them up for this, but I didn't dwell on it. We couldn't go backward. I don't believe that we lost any of their love in the process.

I feel a little impatient. Statistics indicate that more than half of marriages are ending in divorce. I feel sad for our children and for our whole society. The younger generation seems to look at divorce as a solution to problems. I feel they don't fully know what they're doing. Often the reason seems to be "we just grew apart" or "I want it my way and I am unwilling to compromise." Our marriage had its share of stress and difficult circumstances, but we were committed to each other and determined to work things through.

The last twenty years have been times of great change. Economic conditions almost force both parents to work outside the home. The children may become latchkey kids, and family stress increases.

It seems easy to go along day by day and fail to see, or refuse to accept, that professional counsel could prove helpful. Money is spent on everything else, but marriage, the most important human relationship, may be seriously neglected. In some ways I still feel—well, you bring it on yourself. Marriage takes work.

I continue to ask, How can we avoid some of this breakup of families in future generations?

* * *

Doug
Utter shock and very limited feedback made the need to

continue supporting his son a strong challenge.

My initial reaction to our son's decision to divorce was denial. When I found that it was for real, I tried to communicate with him, but it was like talking to a wall. I got no answer. I wrote a letter expounding what I thought was right and wrong for him, which was probably a typical father's reaction. He acknowledged it, but only said it was what he had to do. That's as much explanation as I've had from him. I still don't know why they divorced. We both seemed unable to break through the barriers.

Even though there were no answers, my wife and I knew he wasn't without feelings of affection toward us. We maintained contact in spite of times of real strain. I didn't want him to think that we would turn our backs on him and walk away. He knew that everyone in the family disapproved of his decision, but we kept hanging in there, telling him that we loved him.

I accepted the divorce a lot faster than Laura. There was nothing I could do about it—they're grownups; it's their lives. I prayed that the best thing that could happen in this circumstance would happen. When I could get my oar in the water to help or support, I would and did, but basically it was out of my hands.

Healing came sooner for me than for Laura. She didn't want to move on. She wanted to get the situation fixed. I tried to support her because I knew that she was really struggling with it. But . . . well, life has to go on. You can't stay stuck in this spot forever. You might as well just start moving on.

* * *

Wayne

A quiet man experienced overwhelming grief and yet resolved to support with love.

I felt my son and daughter-in-law's marriage was an excellent relationship between two mature young people. They had chosen well. They had known adventure and many happy times together, but I sensed something was wrong. From the perspective of our longstanding marriage, a breakup was hard for us to anticipate or understand. Finally connecting via phone, I regretfully learned, "Dad, our marriage is in trouble and we are thinking of getting a divorce."

I was stunned. I went immediately to my wife's workplace to inform her. We were both just devastated, and we couldn't believe that they would go through with it. Hazel was just out of it for a few days, not able to think or function. I went to work, but I was just going through the motions. I'm not one to express my feelings easily, but I was really hurting too. It was a few days before we could get the focus off ourselves and our shock and think about our son and what he must be feeling. Our son came for a visit after a short time, and we appreciated his forthrightness, although we didn't get an answer to the question "Why?"

We loved our daughter-in-law, and it's hard to let our relationship with her drift away. We did a lot of speculating about the reasons: accumulation of small hurts, lifestyle changes, her frequent work-related travel, growing differences in values, lack of unity in Christian faith in spite of being reared in Christian homes—but we just didn't know. We kept writing letters and making phone calls to keep in touch with our son, but it was a while before we had a letter from our daughter-in-law trying to explain that they had just "drifted apart." I was glad that Hazel was able to express her feelings in her journal and work through to a place of acceptance.

Fortunately there were no children to be hurt by this decision. My work demanded my attention. Though I was hurting both for myself and for my son, I had to let it go.

✳　　✳　　✳

Russell

Russell did not have a problem forgiving his son, but he did struggle with forgiving himself and setting boundaries for involvement.

My response is probably quite different from that of parents who have participated in a child's marriage that they were pleased with, and that they had hopes and dreams for, then had it torn away. Betty and I had only minimal knowledge of our children's relationships before they married. We did not hold much hope for their success. When the first marriage ended in divorce, it was almost a relief.

I told my son, as the third marriage appeared to be in trouble, "I feel I have some knowledge about you and life, some feelings, and even wisdom that I would be happy to share if I am asked, but I am unwilling to be a dumping place for endless rehash of your current marital difficulties."

It was painful, but I had to create a boundary for myself. I wanted a safe place for him to go, but I couldn't be that safe place because it was all one way, his way.

I never saw forgiveness as something I either had to work through or needed to give. Knowing that the marriages were faulty from the beginning, my sense was one of sorrow, sometimes compassion, but not unforgiveness. Any anger that I had was because of the chaos and turmoil that was injected into our lives.

Guilt sometimes followed for what I might have been as a father to my son. I realize that my guilt was a reflection of family-of-origin issues over which I had no control. For years I had blamed myself for my child's failures. But I did the best I could in raising him, and I can't stay in that self-incrimination stance forever. I have been learning to forgive myself and set boundaries.

If he wants to screw up, that's his problem. I've given him what I can. He doesn't even want what I've got to give now, so why should I fuss about it?

It doesn't take the pain away, though.

How do I go about moving on? Well, denial is the unhealthy way. I get caught in that sometimes, but I'm learning a more healthy way. When the kettle gets to boiling, I find a male friend to talk over my situation with, let the steam escape and find a fresh way of looking at things.

There is a lot in life you can't control. You can stay stuck in those things, or you can choose to find a way to fill your life with things that bring meaning and fulfillment. I value the principle in Philippians 4:8: "Whatever is true, whatever is noble, whatever is right, whatever is pure, whatever is lovely, whatever is admirable—if anything is excellent or praiseworthy—think about such things." I can choose to do this thought or mood exchange.

The good Lord knows life is crummy, and he has offered us a marvelous exchange system: You find your life by giving it away to others. That does not mean denying yourself to the point where you put your own well-being or your family's in jeopardy. There must be balance. These principles have been helpful for me.

*   *   *

Chris

This dad learned that thinking positively can set you up for disaster!

You don't observe your children's marriages and anticipate difficulty. You put a favorable light on everything that you see. Parents like to feel they taught their children responsibility and commitment.

We had no foreknowledge of problems in our daughter's marriage. No perception of any difficulties at all. Nothing. No unusual circumstances. No abuse or drinking, nothing of that nature. All of a sudden she just didn't want to be married. She pulled the plug—she moved out! I feel that she reacted precipitously and took a major step that prevented any kind of reconciliation.

Our first attempts at communication with her were very strained. She anticipated that we wouldn't understand. I told her that we loved her but that she was right, we *didn't* understand. I also told her, "The option you took is not acceptable to us. Your mom and I experienced troubles and difficulties in our marriage, but we worked it through." If they had worked on their differences while they were still together, then I would have been more hopeful, but there is too much to retrace and too much loss of face now that they have separated.

My wife held on to so much anger as she listened to her daughter's immature reasoning and lame excuses. Like so many parents, she felt that our children hadn't sufficiently considered how the decision to divorce would affect their young children.

I'm trying to get away from outright anger. I feel concern, disgust, some guilt, some wondering. Why were our values rejected?

That's where guilt enters in. It's a major feeling on my part. Certainly we did what we considered was right at the time; looking back, we probably couldn't have done things any differently. Or could we? We have to live in the now—and I don't want to accept this present reality. I'm groping. I don't feel I can withdraw from our daughter. She's ours, and she needs love from somewhere, and it's got to come from us—as difficult as it is.

I've spent a lot of thought and emotional energy trying to *fix it,* at least in my own mind. My rest gets disturbed when imaginary conversations seep into my thoughts. I'm also concerned for our parents, who have taken this break so hard.

At least we have been able to be honest with our friends, telling them when we felt rotten and why. I'm at the time of my life when I'm not going to play games with people. If people don't like the way I feel, or Jane doesn't like what I say, or vice versa, that's too bad, because we accept each other as we are, and hopefully others will accept us. Yet how can we get to the point where we can be this open with our daughter? What do we do if she wants to come home for Christmas? We're still too tied to our hurt at this point. I don't know that we even *want* to be available, and that makes me feel even more guilty.

Jane and I have pulled together and become closer as we have walked through this crisis. Hopefully time will help as we work through to forgiveness and resolution and move on.

*   *   *

Tom

Tom felt responsible to see his son's marriage succeed. They were young and he had tried to be helpful, but . . .

When our daughter-in-law moved out, our son came asking, "Dad, why didn't you question me about being so young when I talked about getting into marriage? I think I would have listened."

We could never sit either one of them down and discuss the problems they were having. In spite of our efforts, the marriage failed. I felt I had let God down in some way, as well as the young couple. I guess it was a false guilt.

The first marriage was followed by a second, which, after a few years, began to have problems as well. I tried to give more assistance, responding to calls for help, but I was disappointed when they failed to be honest about their real problems. They shut us off and the world out. We sincerely tried to complete our commitment to them, but I began to feel distrustful and manipulated. If they couldn't be honest with me, I don't know if a neutral, objective counselor would have made a difference.

I wasn't angry and am not angry now, just heartsick over the fractured family and the fact that for almost an entire year our grandchildren have input from only one side of their extended family. It is such a tragedy.

* * *

Don

Don was pulled apart trying to give wise counsel to his son and his wife—which he was asked to do—and to demonstrate unconditional love at the same time.

Our son married after a rocky courtship. There was much discord, and occasionally I was asked for counsel and help in resolving differences. I felt that he was a frequent contributor to their unhappiness and that if he would make some changes things could work out. And I told him so, which didn't make him very happy!

After years of turmoil, they divorced. Instead of being relieved that the conflict was over and he could begin again, our son felt total personal failure. His ego was crushed; he was unable to accept and learn from his mistakes and then go forward.

But gradually, with the help of professional counsel, he rebuilt his self-esteem and sense of hope and new direction. I've come to admire some of the ways he used his and his wife's immaturity and turmoil to teach his kids about love and healthy relationships. Little was hidden from them. They talked about what had been missing in the family and about how they could all learn to respond to each other in more loving ways. Our grandchildren have remained close to each other and to both of their parents.

My work was so demanding during this period that it took some of my focus off my son's marital turmoil. It was a real stab at times, when we were in the middle of it, but there were times when we could walk away from it for a while.

I still find myself hanging on to some anger and unforgiveness, and I'm not sure that I want to do anything about it. I feel semi-justified. I'm not proud of it, but that's the reality. I could almost say that I enjoy it: in this terrible wrong I'm the most right! Now that our son has remarried, there is no longer any hope of resolving everything. There will always be some scars. I have some concern that my resentment, mild or medium, could damage me, but I feel that the Lord will heal me as I attempt to stay close to him.

Ninety percent of my ability to keep on an even keel came from knowing that Muriel and I were seeing eye to eye. We were supporting each other. Another source of personal support was our small group. These friends helped us verbalize our hurts, prayed with us, loved us and helped us gain perspective.

*   *   *

Dennis

This dad cared about both of his children, but living far away made involvement more complicated.

We had never had a chance to build much of a relationship with our son-in-law, due to military service and geographic distance. When we knew that our daughter had done as much as she could to work things through but was unable to resolve the difficulties in their marriage, we had to let it be. They're old enough to know what they want to do. As far as I was concerned, there wasn't any great period of grieving over it, it was just one of those things that was too bad. I wasn't surprised when it happened, because of their circumstances.

But then a second child informed us that there had been a separation. You don't want to go through it again. I wrote letters to give advice, urging them to get counseling and help in reconciling. "You don't understand, Dad," was my son's response. His sincere effort to get things worked out was unsuccessful. I helped him get good legal advice so there would not be prolonged conflict. At least I could do that.

It wasn't until the divorce was final that we were told that it was infidelity on the part of our daughter-in-law that had caused the breakup. Anger, yes—we both felt it, and our son's siblings even more so.

We had not spent a lot of time with our son's wife or had a chance to become close to her. So we were spared some of the intense pain that some parents endure when there has been a close relationship with the in-law child, perhaps for years, before the marriage dissolution. And it was probably easier for us because there were no grandchildren. We would like to have grandchildren, but we wouldn't want them to experience the breakup of their family. Now there can be healing and a fresh start for our son.

*   *   *

Some fathers feel awkward expressing love to their children, yet they feel it intensely. In the emotional turmoil of divorce, it is terribly important for the children and in-law children to *hear* the father's love expressed, either verbally or in writing.

One young man who had been in trouble of many kinds had a dad who never expressed love or affirmation. Finally, in connection with his repaying some borrowed money, he received a note from home—and it was signed, "Love, Dad." That young man carried the note in his wallet for years, until it was literally in shreds. Even a few words can be a treasure.

Hearing their dad's love expressed will strengthen your children and help them move on toward wholeness.

11

The Church's Response

●

YOU HAVE PROBABLY reflected many times on the day your children married. For most of us it was a gathering of loving family and friends who rejoiced in the love our children shared, who witnessed the covenant they made before God to keep the lifelong vows they made to one another. It was a joyous day of celebration, of optimism.

You knew that there would be struggles, hard times as well as good ones, but you trusted that there was a solid understanding of what it means to leave father and mother and become one flesh. You had hope that these two could love each other with sacrificial, supportive, nurturing love.

Now those hopes are dashed, and the wedding pictures are a bittersweet reminder of happier times. Their covenant with God and with each other has been broken. Many of us want to turn for comfort to the institution that gave this marriage its initial blessing: the church.

But can we? Do we feel welcomed, comforted and understood? Or guilty, judged and pushed aside? It will depend on your particular congregation or, at least, your perception of the situation. I know parents who felt like second-class church citizens after their children's marriages failed. They felt that the institutional church criticized their abilities as Christian parents.

Identifying the Old Messages

Our generation, experiencing rampant divorce among our children, is deeply influenced by messages we heard in childhood, messages from a much earlier time:

☐ "I'd never tell my mother if my children divorced, if I could keep from it. It would only hurt her."

☐ "Remarks I heard in childhood, like 'don't go over to the house across the street, that woman is divorced,' stayed with me into my adult years."

☐ "I overheard conversations as a child between my parents and grandmother as she talked about the shame she felt when her youngest child divorced."

These experiences contribute to the attitudes of our generation. We must look at them, realize where they come from and see how they contribute to our responses when our own children divorce. One of the questions that hurting parents have asked me is, "Shouldn't we in the church be correcting this message? Doesn't the church need to be showing the compassion and mercy of Jesus, even when it comes to the brokenness of divorce?" We all are guilty of sin and brokenness of some kind. "If we claim to be without sin, we deceive ourselves and the truth is not in us. If we confess our sins, he is faithful and just and will forgive us our sins and purify us from all unrighteousness" (1 Jn 1:8-9). We want God's grace extended toward us, and so we should extend it toward others. Aren't we called to love each other?

Churches Take a Stand

In an interview with John Westfall, currently pastor of Walnut Creek Presbyterian Church in California, I learned that he had grown up in a church where "there *was* no divorce." It identified itself as a strong family church. Only later did he realize that the reason the church was free of divorce was that when couples began having difficulties in their marriages, they left! The message they got from the church was, "You are no longer acceptable—there is no place for you here."

John tells of this painfully common scenario: "One party of the divorce is singing in the choir, and the other sits in a pew thinking, *Bob [or Mary] is ruining this worship service for me. I can't think of anything except how painful this is.* If they stay in the fellowship and one of the former partners remarries, all three are reminded of their pain while trying to get on with their lives. It happens a lot. Somebody has to leave. They go somewhere else and start a new life. But there is a loss; the person who leaves is cut off from former fellowship and support.

"In that situation you may conclude that the church is not the place to be if you are hurting, only when things are going well, when you have a job, when your life is in order. When you get it back together, then you can come back. But at the moment of pain . . . the church seems to close the door."

Sinners Need Not Apply

Russell grew up in a very conservative church. He felt his church was unwilling to understand or forgive either the divorce of his parents or the actions and divorces of his children. "While it did not alienate me from God and my vital relationship with Jesus Christ, it did cause me to look outside the church for support, for encouragement or for help in solving personal and family problems," he said. That aspect of his life was simply kept separate from his church involvement.

Now Russell and his wife are active in a church that says, "This is a place where you may cry as well as laugh. You can be known—with all of your 'warts,' your 'wayward' children, your griefs and disappointments and guilts. We will pray with you, support you, help you gain perspective and work with you to create wholeness."

John Westfall offers this analysis: "Some of the institutional church is embarrassed about divorce, saying, 'Perhaps we have failed; what happened?' I think there is a sense of powerlessness, and since we don't know what to do, we just ignore it and hope it doesn't personally affect us. We say, 'Oh, that's your private pain.' Nothing should be that way in the body of Christ. The church should be the one place that we deal with divorce realistically and compassionately."

Another pastor, who works with adult ministries in a large church, reflects, "We tend to misinterpret—to believe that if the church is compassionate toward those caught in the brokenness of divorce, by offering divorce recovery workshops, single parenting and blended family classes, it opens the door for laxity toward marriage. But Jesus gives us a model. The scribes and Pharisees had brought to Jesus a woman who had been caught in adultery. They wanted a judgment against her, thus fulfilling the law. Jesus told them that whoever was without sin should cast the first stone. One by one they left. No one remained to condemn her. ' "Neither do I condemn you," Jesus declared. "Go now and leave your life of sin" ' (Jn 8:3-11). In the church we have the opportunity to be part of the redeeming and restorative process of God."

John Stott writes about the tension between the need for high standards that reinforce the biblical covenant of marriage and the New Testament model of grace. Stott points out that we can't forget that in the beginning God created marriage. He created it for the purpose of procreation and also for companionship in which two people nurture and provide for each other and help each other to grow and reach full potential (Gen 2:18). He also intended it to provide a way for this self-giving love to express itself in sexual union (Gen 2:24).[1]

When we realize what God's ideal for marriage was, we become more aware of the tragedy of divorce. Yet even as we oppose divorce, we need to balance our conviction with compassion for each hurting person caught in that tragedy.

What People Long For

In interviews with divorcing individuals, I encountered an outcry for forgiveness, understanding and acceptance—an outcry directed at parents, family and the church. A high percentage of divorced individuals expressed a deep feeling of failure to meet high personal and family expectations based on the biblical standard of marriage. Meeting these expectations has become increasingly difficult in our current society, where the Christian ethic is no longer the norm.

And I got these responses to the question, "Was your church a support to you?"

☐ "No, I was expelled! I finally found another church where I could receive forgiveness, instruction and healing."

☐ "Yes, I was invited to parishioners' homes for an occasional overnight, including Christmas Eve, so that I wouldn't be alone on Christmas Day. I also received ministerial counseling and fellowship by participating in group activities."

☐ "I never came to church before I was separated. I started coming with friends for something to do on weekends. I am learning about God's love and forgiveness, and I found a support group for separated people and then Divorce Recovery. I still need an ongoing Divorce Recovery small group and teaching and guidance while I find my way."

Parents, Scripture and the Church

In interviewing divorced people, I heard this comment:

My mom, like me, went back and forth, wanting to believe that God could heal the marriage. We continued to believe in my husband. When I shared with her the details of both mental and physical abuse, she began to look at it in a different light. She stood by me through the marriage and divorce.

She felt my ups and downs, my pain. She wanted my dream as much as I did. My mother felt angry, sad, confused as I did, and *she never wanted to believe that divorce was the answer.* She continued to seek God's guidance, was touched by God's grace and mercy, and was able to help both of us.

As my friend Laura and I met to help each other deal with our broken families, we both had to examine what we believed about divorce and what the Scriptures taught. Studying together was helpful. We knew that marriage, intended to last a lifetime, was given for the benefit of human beings. We knew its breakdown would bring pain and alienation from one another and from God. Yet sins of pride, selfishness, thoughtlessness, indifference, dishonesty and broken trust, anger and conflict, sometimes even infidelity, abuse and violence accumulate—and divorce occurs. What are parents supposed to do? How should we balance our knowledge of Jesus' offer of compassion and forgiveness, and his instruction for us to do likewise, with some of the biblically based positions of the institutional church?

Throughout history the church has taken various positions concerning marriage, divorce and remarriage:

☐ no divorce and no remarriage

☐ divorce but no remarriage

☐ divorce and remarriage for adultery or desertion

☐ divorce and remarriage under a variety of circumstances

These positions are examined at length in the book entitled *Divorce and Remarriage: Four Christian Views*.[2] This book could prove to be a valuable resource for you as you work through the issues and your thoughts and questions.

In my interviews with more than twenty pastors of different backgrounds, I heard encouraging words. Many churches have come to recognize the depth of the divorce syndrome in our society and attempt to offer practical help. Marriage Encounter and other programs attempt to help couples build better marriages rather than choose divorce. And there seems to be movement toward greater compassion with regard to divorce. "Some branches of the church are bringing these issues more into the open and discussing them in public gatherings where ten years ago this might not have been true," according to one pastor with whom I spoke. He added, "This is done realizing that *accepting the reality of divorce doesn't mean approval of that reality.*"

Letting People Care for Us

"Did you seek professional counsel when your child divorced?" I asked a distraught pastor and father.

"No, but I don't know why we didn't," he replied. "We certainly needed it."

I have found that many in our parenting generation hesitate to seek professional help for themselves. We feel we should be able to solve our own problems. However, it can be very helpful to have another person assist us in sorting out what issues are causing our distress. An empathetic pastor can provide counsel and a listening ear or can suggest a therapist with experience in family counseling.

Another way to care for yourself is through small groups that offer support, model openness, and give you a chance to express your feelings and ask your questions. The group can act as an extended family, provide ongoing prayer and understanding and help with the rebuilding of trust in relationships.

I'm so thankful that there are people in the church who are willing to say, "I value you enough to really share who I am with you." I know that this can happen, for Karl and I have experienced it over the years in two ways. First, we were part of a couples' support group. We were one of five couples who had diverse family needs: children with serious physical or emotional challenges, heavy pastoral responsibilities, divorcing children and other needs. We met weekly for ten years to study God's Word, encourage one another in spiritual growth and give practical help where possible. We experienced the joy of fellowship each week as we shared a meal and prayerfully tried to support one another in the big and little things of our daily lives.

And second, we found support in a surprising place: with a small group of university student leaders in our church with whom we had the role of "older friends." These young people shared their personal struggles week by week—and we couldn't sit among them and pretend that there was no pain in our own lives. We felt a strong imperative to be honest, so we talked about the pain of our children's divorces. The students were a tremendous source of love and prayerful support for both of us at a time of personal turmoil. Now, years later, we still have vital relationships with many of these young people, most of whom have married and begun families of their own.

I continue to see how helpful it is to have models in the church—people who are willing to be real, to honestly tell their stories from the past and the present, to share how to handle failures and weaknesses with grace. Perhaps you can take initiative to start a group or class in your church to help others who are going through divorce in their families.

Last year, Laura and I led a workshop called "Parents' Response to Divorce" at a women's conference sponsored by our church. It proved to be helpful not only to mothers with divorcing children but also to friends of families where divorce was occurring—and to divorced daughters who wanted to get a better sense of what their parents might be feeling.

If your church doesn't have a small group ministry, perhaps you can lead the way! (See chapter eleven.)

Learning to Care for Others

Having experienced the pain of family breakup, we can help our churches learn how to be families where brothers and sisters care for one another and give support and encouragement as well as holding high standards for marriage.

Don is the father of grown daughters, but he began teaching three-year-old boys and girls in the Sunday school several years ago. He had a desire to give some attentive, loving, masculine input into the lives of kids who, because of divorce and other reasons, have little influence from their fathers. He enjoys it so much that he continues to be involved and has recruited other men to join him in this vital ministry to children.

My friends Mavon and Janet, both mothers and grandmothers, have spent a number of years teaching fifth-grade girls in Sunday-school classes. They keep close track of these girls as they advance through junior high and high school. They listen to their joys and their disappointments, to their sorrow when parents are divorced. And they pray both for them and with them. They have found an effective way of creating extended family in the life of the church.

Many single parents long to be included in ordinary activities with other families as well as outings and celebrations. Because you and I have experienced some isolation, we can reach out to others with true understanding. Can you choose to extend yourself to a family in this way, to show them practical, unconditional love?

Helping Our Churches Care

Darrel Young, adult ministries director at University Presbyterian Church in Seattle, shared the following insight in a conversation with me:

As we look at the needs in our culture, we can be preoccupied with the endless questions of "Who's right and who's wrong? Who has failed and who hasn't?"

Instead we might better ask, "How can the church be redemptive and healing in an increasingly wounded and wounding society?" Not only is divorce a sign that deep wounding has happened; divorce *creates* wounds.

Fifty to sixty percent of the kids in our schools will live in a single-parent home. Before we judge the divorcing, we must consider whom we exclude by such judgment.

Where will these kids go to learn "family" if not to the church? Where will the single parent go for support, healing and nurturing and direction if not to the church?

The challenge for the church is to strongly uphold marriage while also offering compassion, practical help and teaching when brokenness occurs.

As I talk with parents, we agree that there is a lot to know and learn about commitment in marriage and family relationships. It may be difficult to begin to be more open with one another in the church, to learn about healthy conflict resolution and forgiveness and trust, but the rewards are tremendous. There comes a time when we have the opportunity, as I have said before, to exercise choice and make a decision to hang in there, to stay in our own marriages, to stand by our kids regardless of their marital decisions. We can gather resource people to help enrich our own marriages and to help single parents, blended families, and those who are living through separation and divorce.

Classes for teens and preteens could include teaching on honesty in relationships, sexual purity and abstinence, respect, forgiveness, interdependence and mutual support in family life. Such classes would be especially beneficial if the teachers were demonstrating loving family life and good marriages.

We need modeling of good, long-term marriages, healthy communication patterns and conflict resolution within the life of the church. Our pastors and leaders need to be honest, to be real with us about the stresses and strains of the marriage relationship and what it means to be committed. We may not be able to reverse our children's decisions. However, because we have lived through the realities of divorce in the family, we are better equipped to be agents of change. We can encourage our churches to help other pilgrims on this road to wholeness.

Stephen Ministries is a national program that trains laypeople in effective caring and listening skills to enable them to come alongside someone in crisis. It is intended to be support, not counseling. A "Stephen Minister" can provide a listening ear for a parent trying to work through the shock of a child's decision to divorce. Reaching out to others can bring perspective and healing for yourself. You might want to become involved and get such training yourself.[3]

Are there ongoing marriage enrichment classes in your church? They can teach good relational skills and provide a supportive network as well. Some churches provide support for families where divorce is occurring or has occurred. This support may take various forms:

☐ Divorce-recovery programs that help individuals through their pain and rejection. Such programs can be a first step in reconciling non-Christians with their Lord as well as themselves.

☐ Classes and groups that encourage and support single parents.

☐ Programs for blended families that bring insight for the particular needs that occur with stepparenting.

☐ Summer camps that mix single-parent families with two-parent families and support parents and children alike. The one-parent family gets a "normal" camp experience, and the single parent gets a chance to be with other adults while the kids are in supervised recreation or crafts classes.

☐ Support groups for children of divorce where young people can come knowing they will be understood. Such groups can also provide guidance and information about resources to meet particular needs.

One such group was formed in my church for teens from divorced families. Called "Second Wind," it is facilitated by leaders who can speak from personal experience of divorce in their families, who know what it feels like when a young person says, "I just hate it when they . . ." These leaders can offer empathy but also the perspective of time and healing. In addition, there are leaders who come out of strong Christian families where long-term marriage has been the model. There is time to teach about long-term commitment, honest loving communication in relationships and sexual purity before marriage.

Second Wind is not an ongoing weekly group. The leaders try to be sensitive to where the teens in the church "are at." When the need arises, this group meets for several weeks, giving very specific support. Later it may sponsor a day-long seminar to deal with certain needs. Both formats have proved effective.

If we in the Christian church are to represent the family of God to the culture around us, we need to do all we can to be a family to one another, to strongly support committed marriages and yet to demonstrate compassion for families where breakdown has occurred and to help in every way we can.

12

Gaining Perspective Through Small Groups

●

I REMEMBER STANDING at the kitchen sink thinking, "I can't get through this alone!"

At a time of personal crisis, we need other people who know from experience what we are encountering and can respond to our turmoil with genuine understanding and empathy. We need someone who can say—and mean it—"I know just how you feel."

This kind of support can come through the friendship of one special person or, better yet, be spread over the broader base of a small group. If you open your heart to just one friend, you may run the risk of placing that person under too great a burden. A larger perspective and varied experiences can give helpful support. I have already mentioned the value of a group's support; in this chapter we will take a closer look.

My own journey into wholeness was encouraged through friendships in a "general" small group. But I also sought out Laura, who knew from experience what my questions and feelings were in the specific area of divorce in the family. She was willing to share her pilgrimage. We began by recounting our stories and exchanging excerpts from our journals.

When Laura and I were ready to expand our understanding, we called others. Seven concerned Christian parents from various backgrounds, with similar values, met together at our invitation. Through the years we had all loved and prayed for our children. We had been actively involved with them in school, sports, community and church activities. Now we were mature, some of us were grandparents—how time had sped.

We had something else in common. Our children were going through, or had gone through, divorce. *Divorce* was an unwelcome word which we were reluctant to say aloud in reference to our own children. As we shared this fact and explored its impact on all our lives, we were careful not to intrude, and we gave group members permission to pass when any question felt invasive.

First we asked, "How did you hear about the separation and divorce, and what was your response to it? What were some of the things that you did, initially, as a result?" Laura shared her own story while the rest of us thought about what our answers would be.

Other questions followed, aiding the discussion:

☐ Has there been a history of divorce in your family?

☐ How did you cope or are you coping with the news?

☐ Do you blame yourself?

☐ What do you think were contributing factors to the marriage breakdown?

☐ What became the most important focus of concern in your response to your children?

☐ What were some of the practical things you did?

☐ How did you take care of yourself in the midst of this crisis?

☐ What enabled you to keep your balance and perspective?

☐ Who offered support to you: extended family, friends, pastor, neighbors?

Expressing our common hurt led to healing as we realized that we all shared feelings of anger, disbelief, sadness, pain, confusion and guilt. It helped to talk with others who could understand.

Some of us had never spoken openly about our pain before. It was easier than expected, and we left feeling less burdened. I believe that God was with us to help us take a step forward. While this did not lead to an ongoing small group, it gave support for a specific time and purpose.

Even if you are in a "general" small group or have supportive individual friends, you may find a group focused on the adjustments in the family surrounding divorce to be helpful for a period of time.

Getting Started

Finding a small group can be a challenge. Many churches encourage them, though, often in the form of classes or support groups. If none exist in your church or if you are not a part of a church family, consider reaching out to one or two other people in similar circumstances and starting one. The early church gathered regularly in each other's homes to pray, study the Scriptures, have fellowship, share a simple meal and support one another by sharing their lives and praying for each other's needs. They didn't have professionals to help them. They just did it. Remember Sydney? She advertised in the paper.

How to form a support group:

☐ Find another person to help you get started. It's hard to be a Lone Ranger. Share your ideas and hopes. Pray together for guidance.

☐ Make a list of people who might benefit and some who might be further down the road in coping with divorce in their families.

☐ Start calling people. A group of six to eight is ideal, but it may take additional contacts to find that many who are seriously interested.

☐ Establish a time and place to meet. The privacy of a home might be best. Plan far enough ahead to allow people to arrange their schedules.

☐ At your initial meeting, discuss your ideas. Include the input of the others. Be sure everyone shares ideas so that you can agree on your purpose. Then determine who wants to continue.

Getting Organized

Each member of a small group needs to understand the purpose and agree on some basics.

1. What is our purpose? An example: to share the experience of our children's divorce, learn from each other, and seek to grow and learn in ways that honor God.

2. When will we meet—how often and how long each time?

3. How many times will we meet before we evaluate our commitment? At the time of evaluation, it is understood that anyone may discontinue participation if his or her needs are not met.

4. Where shall we meet? Using the same place each time may be easiest, or you may prefer to rotate homes. If refreshments are to be served, who will be responsible? (Keep it simple.)

5. How will the group be led? You may choose your leader from the group. Leadership may be rotated, or you may want one trained leader to do it regularly if you haven't had small-group experience before.

6. What will the format be? (Open in prayer, use a book or

topic for discussion, share from our own lives, spend time in supportive prayer for one another, or whatever.)

7. Should the group include both men and women?

8. What will our ground rules be regarding confidentiality?

9. Will we be an open group (new people may join anytime) or closed (with an original number that stays constant for the agreed number of weeks)?

Rules That Help

The following "rules" have been formulated partly from my personal experience and partly from unpublished work done by Tim Snow, a pastor at University Presbyterian Church in Seattle.

Because of the focus on family life and hurt, it is important that the group agree on some ground rules.

Commitment to the group is essential. We are less likely to share significant issues from our lives with people we hardly know or folks who are not willing to stick around through the hard times as well as the joyful ones. Meeting together must have a high priority; members should agree not to skip meetings unless there's a very important reason.

Confidentiality must be maintained. Trust is the basis for sharing our lives with each other. If trust is broken, it takes a long time to rebuild. We must assume that everything we say in the group is private and can be shared outside the group only with specific permission. If we seek prayer support from others outside the group, it must be only in very general terms. Confidentiality is essential for the health and staying power of a small group.

Listening is an art. The members of the group should be careful to listen to one another, not jump in to solve problems. Giving advice and help too soon, even with concern and compassion, can cut off communication. It takes time to empathize and explore people's feelings. It is important to suppress our desire to fix things or remove the pain when someone shares a problem. Down the road there may be a request for our help in solving a problem, but it comes after good listening.

Also, agree that each of you will speak only for yourself. When spouses (or group members) speak for each other, it may indicate unclear boundaries. Refrain from speaking for others in the group, even though you may think you know what they would say.

Getting Going

The first step is to get to know one another and start building a basis for trust. One tool for getting acquainted is simply to ask a question each person can answer: something about your background, where you come from, the members of your family, your vocational interests, the things that you like to do and that bring you joy. You might try one or two such questions in your initial meeting to give everyone an opportunity to participate in a nonthreatening way. You could make a sharing question part of your regular format while you are getting acquainted.

If you are meeting as a Christian group, I encourage you always to include prayer. In it you recognize the Lord, a power beyond yourself, a Person with whom you can share your concerns, joys, lack of faith, anything. In the beginning you might repeat the Lord's Prayer, which is familiar and powerful. Because there are different usages, some saying "debts" and others "trespasses" or sins, agree on one wording beforehand to avoid awkwardness. You might prefer to write a prayer to use as you open your time together, one that addresses the group's specific goals.

A small-group setting is also a good place to try conversational prayer: several people offer short prayers of a sentence or two concerning one topic or person, each building on what the last person has mentioned, as in normal conversation. When one topic has been covered, the next can be introduced and prayed for briefly by a number of people. This helps to eliminate repetition and formality. I suggest an honest, informal style as you talk to God. Some members may need to be encouraged or given freedom just to listen until it feels comfortable to take part.

Sydney said that she could not enter into her Christian counseling group's prayer time for two months because she had built such a wall of defense. She did not feel pressure to participate but instead sensed an acceptance till she was ready. It is important to create this kind of atmosphere.

Small-Group Challenges

A small group is a perfect place to affirm others. We don't often take time to let people know that they are loved, to tell them what we see as their gifts and talents. But each of us needs to know we have value and to be reminded that God treasures us as his child and is concerned about the things that concern us. It is a privilege to affirm others.

In any small group there may come times to be firm in love. You've all observed the one who dominates the conversation or who insists on his own way. Sometimes a member of a group who is uncomfortable with the depth of emotion or the subject being shared either sidetracks the conversation or makes jokes, defeating the communication process. Another person may have such overwhelming needs that a therapy group would be more appropriate for him or her. If your group includes one or more of these individuals, the group leader or facilitator may need to speak to them privately to help them establish more helpful communication patterns for the good of all. Also, the leader may need to consult with a pastor, Stephen Minister or trained counselor if the group process is repeatedly being sabotaged.

We need to remember that each group participant brings along his or her own theological and cultural presuppositions, family value system, relationship to the divorcing child and spouse, and patterns of communication by which to approach conflict and blame. Not all have the same starting point: a divorce is seen by some as a tragedy, by others as an unwanted solution, by others as a difficult change requiring adjustment.

Looking at the Emotional Issues

Remember that you are meeting to learn from each other (sharing experiences and feelings, not deep interpretations which are more appropriate for therapy groups) and to grow in ways that honor God. Growth occurs by first becoming aware of your true emotions in the face of your circumstances and joining with others who are addressing the same issues. Those who met with Laura and me were encouraged by the realization that others experienced similar emotional responses.

It may be helpful to select a topic to focus your discussion:

☐ How does divorce fit into my family history and my religious beliefs?

☐ Do I have feelings of guilt? Do I question my parenting skills?

☐ Do I feel ashamed? Am I afraid to face my friends?

☐ How have I responded to the young people's behavior changes and rejection of our family's values? What are possible alternative responses?

☐ I feel such a sense of grief and loss of my former son- or daughter-in-law. How can I manage this and move on?

☐ Can I remain friends with my in-law child and still be loyal to my child? How can I show loyalty to my child even when I believe he or she is the basic problem?

☐ How can I handle my pain when my children experience

deep sorrow, anger or despair?

□ I am anxious over the demands on my own emotional resources. What are some ways to lessen this?

□ What is going to happen to my grandchildren? How can I help them? Will I get to see them if they move away?

□ How can I help my kids? I'm so frustrated trying to understand what to do.

Looking at the Practical Issues

Each of us (the extended family as well as the parents) must work through and accept the changes in the family structure. Discussion with others in similar circumstances helps us to evaluate our own situation, to get a clearer look at where we want to be and possibly how to get there.

"Divorce brings a family face to face with old, unresolved issues. It is a unique opportunity for growth, amidst the pain and trauma," says Tresa Wilbee Wiggins in her study "Divorce and the Extended Family Member."[1] She offers some questions for consideration.

□ How much are we willing to rearrange our own schedules and lifestyles in order to help?

□ When does our help become counterproductive and need to be terminated? How will we know when to quit?

□ How will we handle the tension if economic necessity forces divorced offspring to move in with us? How have others coped with loss of privacy, differences over the discipline of grand-children and setting of "house rules"?

□ How can we stay close to our grandchildren, particularly if, as paternal grandparents, we see them less often now because mothers usually end up with primary custody?

□ Our divorcing children sometimes have very strong emo-tional responses to their circumstances. They need to be supported even though we may not approve or feel comfort-able with those emotions. How can we accomplish this?

Personal Growth Issues

When we have become aware of our emotional responses to divorce and have started to deal with the practical matters that arise, we are challenged to ask:

□ What can I learn from this change or crisis?

□ How can my own marriage be enriched? Do some things need to change?

□ Am I living out Christian values? Where do I go from here?

□ Can I learn and grow in the midst of this trauma and pain?

□ Do I have the emotional resources to meet the challenges?

We must recognize the limitations of a small group. It offers opportunity for discussion and candid sharing, but it can't solve all the challenges that divorce brings to our families. It *can* offer a safe place to express our emotions and find empathy. And it may become a sounding board as we explore possible solutions for practical issues we face.

We may think we have some answers as to what our children should do—but they are probably not asking our opinion! Meanwhile, we may be very confused about what we ourselves should be doing. Sometimes a professional family counselor can help us explore specific questions and issues. But friends, pastors and counselors can only counsel. We are the ones who must take action: we must seek God's counsel for ourselves and our own lives and act upon the knowledge we are being given, knowing we are not alone (Mt 28:20). We have the opportunity to take steps to open up—to *choose* to be more transparent about our questions and needs with those close to us. And then we can trust that respectful transparency will bring us the rewards of perspective, growth and joy.

13

Refreshed and Renewed

●

IN THE MIDST OF ongoing daily frustrations or pressures or pain, it is important to find ways to rest. Learning to see the beauty in small things, whether sharing a walk in the park with a friend or viewing a flaming sunset, can give us rest from the tense and unhappy circumstances we sometimes must live in. Pursuing a hobby can absorb our minds and bodies. Reaching out to help others allows us to look beyond our own troubles. Journaling our circumstances and our feelings about them can allow us to see and choose what is important—and to lay aside the unimportant. Activities can be like breathing fresh air after being in a stuffy room: they allow us to go on with new energy.

Recording the Past and Present
In the Old and New Testament Scriptures, we often find the

Israelites being encouraged to look back and remember the faithfulness of God. In the eleventh chapter of Hebrews the writer tells about one hero after another, reminding the people how God was faithful in each circumstance. Remembering helped them to stand fast in adversity.

We are no different. It is good for us to look back through our personal and family history, recalling the ways in which God has enabled us and brought us joy and the people who have supported and encouraged us.

In my family's period of change and trauma, my journal became an invaluable friend to whom I could write my innermost thoughts, both good and bad. It offered a safe place to explore my feelings, to sort out ideas, to record celebrations, conversations and times of joy—and to be reminded of God's faithfulness in the past. And it gave me a place to think about what I desired to do and become in the days ahead.

Our children's decisions to divorce brought about strong emotional responses. There was often confusion between what I *should* do and what I *wanted* to do. I needed to become fully aware of my own feelings so I could take responsibility for them and then could move forward in healthy and loving ways.

It was helpful to realize that I was on a journey that was not only physical and emotional but also spiritual. I needed to move through the denials to discover who I really was. I needed to look at my limitations, my sorrow and my pain— and also at what brought me joy and what gifts I had to share. Only then could I set some attainable goals.

Knowing I was called not only to love God and myself but also to love others, I became particularly aware of needing to love our children and grandchildren. But first I needed to know the truth about myself. Then I could keep the good that I saw and throw away the garbage (unreasonable standards, prejudice, blame, shame, unforgiveness and old hurts).

When I discovered personal weaknesses and failures I could confess them to God and move on, forgiven, into new and more wholesome attitudes.

Why I Journal

My journal has been a chronicle of circumstances and responses. In addition to writing down happenings and how I am responding to them, I record some night dreams; I put in some descriptive writing exercises which provide a refreshing diversion; I include some of my current prayers.

Journaling has helped me become more organized and more focused on what needs to be done. It provides space to talk to God, to listen to him and to record insights that come from times of reflection and times of reading Scripture.

My journal provides a way to see more of the world around me. It can be a diversion when I need to refocus my thoughts, when I am discouraged or sad. I sometimes sit in the garden (in other places too) and try to describe, in great detail, the things all around me—shapes, colors, the textures of leaves, the movement of insects and so on. Getting lost in observing and describing beauty becomes a refreshing minivacation.

It's sometimes helpful to ask questions in my journal. *What keeps me from believing in myself? Can't I believe that God will guide me in this circumstance?*

Sometimes when I am aware of an intense emotion, I ask, *If that sting in my heart could speak, what would it say to me?* Letting my God-given imagination run to create a dialogue, I gain insight into my emotional responses.

I make lists of the things for which I am thankful. I record dreams for the coming year. I've learned to write down these ideas and number them in order of priority. This book grew out of just such an exercise. It was exciting to let the ideas flow and not say to myself, *You can't do that!* Many of the thoughts and insights for this book had their origins in Laura's

nd my journals. Yet I had begun journaling primarily as a tool
)f self-discovery—never suspecting I would need it for sur-
·ival during my children's divorces.

I have excerpted a few entries from my journal:

I have been reading Madeleine L'Engle's book *Circle of
Quiet* this week. Some of the things she writes about
creativity and the Holy Spirit and about self-image got me
to thinking.

For years, since I learned about God's desire to heal our
memories, I have been praying for him to do that in my life
and to help me share the concept with others in the context
of workshops and personal counseling. Today I was challenged by a new thought—at least it was not fully formed
before—that I could offer to God my self-image with all its
quirks, false concepts, truths and half-truths. I have done
this as I sat here on the patio in the filtered sunshine,
surrounded by God's beauty in our garden, quietly supported by Karl as he napped in the lawn chair. In the
background my neighbor's child was filling the air with
melody as she played the piano.

Heavenly Father, I offer to you the image that I call
myself. It has been built by circumstances, parental values,
words and challenges, personal choices and many forces
that I recognize as both good and sometimes evil, lifting me
but sometimes tearing me down as well. Some of the mirror
of myself is true, some false and twisted and surely limited.

Please, Father, take it all and heal it—correct what is
false, and replace it with your truth, through the ministry of
your Holy Spirit. Bring into my consciousness the image of
myself that *you* want me to see—one that reflects the
resources that you have created within me but that have
been overshadowed and covered by childhood as well as
adult hurts. Father, please remember to be gentle as you
replace the long-held props, the excuses for inertia, with

your strengths and creative force and give me courage to look and see the truth.

* * *

Shortly after the divorce:

My mood is much better today as I realize once again how important it is to let go of my concerns and just trust in God's love. The heaviness of worry makes me gloomy, and it wears me out. But I've realized something new: When I worry I am trying to keep control. Does this in some way limit God's freedom to move? Much better, I think, to turn everything over to him and *let go.*

* * *

A dialogue with God:

Heavenly Father, you know what is in both Laura's and my hearts. For myself there is a real desire to be a godly woman in this set of circumstances, and yet so much of the time I flounder, unable to understand what specific actions would be helpful and constructive. Could some of our struggles and small resolutions be helpful to others who are also in this place? What have I learned through this pain? Anything?

You've learned that love is strong but doesn't override free choice. You've learned that you aren't responsible to "fix it." You've learned that forgiveness is a daily requirement on your part.

I don't know the rules anymore. I've had nineteen years in the position of a mother-in-law bonded to daughters-in-law, and now all of a sudden I am being called by my first name and am supposed to be something else—*what?* What role do they want me to fill? How far do I carry loyalty to my own child?

Are you really seeking my answers?

I sometimes am, but it's easier to complain and focus on the past and not address the reality of the present with you, Father. Please forgive my weakness when I seek to find the answers within myself. It's hard not to feel failure as a parent and not to feel self-pity as a hurting person.

*   *   *

After a lunchtime conversation:

I had a long conversation with Hazel on her lunch hour yesterday. We were talking about our journaling experiences. I was sharing with her about Steve Hayner's recent sermon on praise and about the imprecatory psalms of David—that so many of them express fear and anger and vindictive feelings, and yet all of the psalms of the Old Testament are considered psalms of praise. Then she said, with a look of new understanding on her face, "That's just what we do with our journaling, isn't it? We first get in touch with our emotions: hurtful, fearful, angry, resentful and vindictive, and gradually we work through to peace and perspective and eventually to forgiveness and thankfulness."

It's similar to the process David expresses in the psalms. Two spiritual realities can't occupy the same place, just as two material things can't occupy the same space. First, we have to see our spiritual condition as it actually is; then we have to offer it to God; only then can his truth come in as a replacement. Love cannot exist in the same place that is occupied by anger or hatred or fear.

Escape the Pressure

We frequently get entangled in our swirling thoughts about a problem situation, and they exhaust us. Sitting with your journal, focusing on what you see around you and describing it in detail, you can break the pattern. Remember that familiar advice: "Whatever is true, whatever is noble, whatever is right, whatever is pure, whatever is lovely, whatever is admirable—if anything is excellent or praiseworthy—think about such things" (Phil 4:8).

One day I wrote:

I have seated myself in the lawn chair in the garden, where the long shadows of the budding apple tree cross my notebook and run up the kitchen wall, reminding me of murals, so carefully detailed. A breeze dances through the yard, ruffling new, soft, yellow-green leaves of the birch, and in the neighbor's yard a robin chirps its familiar call.

How beautiful the garden is, with new delicate leaves on the Japanese maple that hangs over the corner of the fence, draping it with a lacy canopy. Peeping underneath are magenta and rose magnolia blossoms with creamy ivory centers.

A single petal floats silently to the ground. A bee buzzes by my head on its way to the apple blossoms. As I look I am refreshed.

Luci Shaw on Journaling

Early in my experience with journaling, I attended a workshop led by Luci Shaw, accomplished poet and writer with a strong Christian faith. She had recently lost her husband to a fight with cancer and told us how her journal had been a strong anchor during that painful time. I was deeply appreciative of her suggestions on journaling. I recorded them as follows:

☐ Use a spiral binder 9 1/2 by 6 3/8 inches that lies flat, large enough to write in without balling up your hand but small enough to carry with you. Put your name, address and phone number on the outside, so that if you lose it, it can be returned. Date each entry completely for future reference.

☐ Be absolutely honest. This book is just between you and God.

☐ Find a safe, private place to keep the journal.

☐ Most people are catapulted into journaling by a change in their lives. It might be an engagement, marriage, conception of a child, divorce (your own or your child's) or spiritual renewal that stimulates your reflective thoughts and becomes the impetus for keeping track of your experience.

☐ Journal-keeping is a creative activity that encourages us to observe and describe more precisely. It allows us to find significance in small details of our lives; what seems unsensational often achieves special meaning when we write it down.

☐ Journaling is also therapy. When those chaotic or fragmented thoughts and anxieties seem to be taking control of my thinking I can write them into my journal, creating order from chaos. The words draw the sting out of my heart and reduce it to words that are more manageable.

☐ We are verbal thinkers. In your journal you capture and keep that which would be soon forgotten. What has been fragmented or chaotic in your thinking, a mere glimpse of something real, becomes concrete, approachable and applicable when put into words. Luci said, "In the process of writing we discover what it is that we know."

☐ Journal writing doesn't demand literary professional skills. It's catching and treasuring joyful, crucial or significant moments in your life. Journaling is the act of slowing down enough to write down what we observe, think or feel—and *it's a good thing to be slowed down.*

I agree with Luci Shaw that the process of journaling is more important than the product. Take her hints and mine along with others that you may glean from books or other journalers, and mold them into your own process; create your own style. But don't underestimate the value of having a journal as your friend—a friend who will listen, will never judge, will help you sort out your pain, your prayers, your anger and your hopes in ways you've never dreamed.

Creative Options for Nonjournalers

Journal writing is not the only way to achieve escape and refreshing relaxation. Many of us have hobbies that bring a sense of joy and satisfaction. Bird watching in my garden or on walks through the parks brings me refreshment. It reminds me of the unfathomable creativity of God, and I am thankful.

Painting or sketching can divert pain and absorb us in beauty. Photography can also be very satisfying. Perhaps you have always wanted to try working with clay, to take pottery classes. Would now be a good time? Listening to good music lifts the spirit from the mundane. Using headphones to block out other noises might be a good way to treat yourself.

We are continually bombarded with challenges to make exercise a part of our schedule, and it *is* important in achieving relaxation and health. You may struggle with making it a regular habit, but it has obvious rewards. "Volkswalks" are popular in our area, offering not only exercise but also fellowship if you have that desire. Swimming is one of the best all-round ways to keep your body limber and relaxed. I encourage you to be involved in some form of physical exercise, as a gift to yourself.

Or be creative in finding ways to use your time and energy to help someone else. That can be great therapy for *you*. My blind sister lives in a nursing-care facility. One of the aides, a very cheerful woman, began volunteering her time at the suggestion of her doctor. She had been battling depression. Now, fourteen years later, she is still involved but as part of the staff. "These people are like family to me—I love them," she said. I am so grateful for her thoughtful, encouraging ways, as well as for other volunteers who read to my sister, take her for short walks or just come to visit. When we can give some time to helping people who have much greater challenges than our own, and whose circle of fellowship is so limited, our perspective and balance will be greatly helped.

There are halfway houses for women who need protective care. Some of my friends and I enjoyed taking our sewing baskets to such a shelter once a month to do some mending.

Usually it was to replace a lost button or repair a hem or zipper that had pulled loose. Some of these women were very grateful for such a simple thing, and it brought us joy to be helpful.

Not long after the first divorce hit our family, Karl and I became involved with a young Estonian family who had been driven out of their country because of their Christian faith. The parents and four small children had come to the United States with five suitcases containing all their possessions. Helping them learn how to find their way and function in our city was very rewarding. They needed some tutoring in English, but more pressing was their need to find an adequate place to live, obtain household furnishings and get the children established in school. Becoming involved with this wonderful family, who had suffered much but had faith in God to see them through, was an inspiration to us, And it helped us to have greater joy and perspective about our own pain. (Some of our adventures with this family made their way into my journal and continue to bring me joy.)

Lift your eyes beyond your troubles. Ask the Lord to show you someone to help, some practical ministry of caring that will do the same for you.

14

Where Are You Now?

●

THE TABLES WERE SET; the decorations were in place. The corsages and boutonnieres had been pinned on, and with quickened heartbeat Karl and I began to greet the guests who were arriving to celebrate our fiftieth wedding anniversary.

It was a marvelous opportunity to affirm our immediate family and to celebrate a full life together. Extended family members as far away as California were joined by intimate old-time friends and a few very special young people who had become like adopted sons and daughters. Yet in the midst of overwhelming joy, there were fleeting moments of sadness at the absence of our former daughters-in-law. They too had given us joy, but their presence was not appropriate. Their places had been taken by others. All we could do was rejoice that healing was occurring. We had all moved through the pain to joy and celebration with the two loving women who had become new wives to our sons.

The next day a larger gathering of friends came to share "Coffee Time" with us and to remember the forties. The whole family, including our new daughters-in-law, had a share in preparing this warm party, filled with music. How proud and awed we were by their creativity and love. We felt truly blessed.

As I reflect back on that two-day celebration, I'm reminded that life is bittersweet. How incredible that what seems such a short passage of time has encompassed fifty years. The anniversary was all the more celebrated because of our gratitude and relief that Karl had survived a serious bout with cancer the year before. The fifth decade of our marriage had been the most painful but had also contained some of the richest moments. Karl and I sense a greater mutuality and a deeper level of love from the two sons who have experienced divorce. In addition, I was challenged to learn new skills: keeping medical insurance records and using a computer. It has been very gratifying.

In writing this book I've relived the years of pain that accompanied the dissolution of two marriages. I was forced to look at my emotions and responses, and I didn't always like what I saw. I was forced to think things through and deal with unrealistic expectations, especially the idea that *my* children would always succeed.

The sixties and seventies had been times of great social upheaval, yet I had believed that we would not be adversely affected. But we were. I learned firsthand that trials and personal pain *are* part of life, even for "nice people," even for people who trust God. And I learned that our faithful heavenly Father continues to guide, counsel and support us in the most difficult of life's passages, just as in easier times.

Even during Karl's first battle with cancer, I was faced with writing deadlines that compelled me to focus for significant chunks of time on something other than his disease. When it seemed that nothing was moving for him, I could see forward motion on the manuscript. I was invigorated by a creative flow of energy that produced balance when I desperately needed it—much as I had found release in my journaling, weaving, and, yes, even my angry housecleaning during the darkest days of absorbing the impact of divorce on our lives. As I have been writing these chapters, Karl has learned of renewed malignancy and we are facing a new round of treatment. Another time of fear; another time to find creative release; another chance to learn to rest in God's promise: "The eternal God is your refuge, and underneath are the everlasting arms" (Deut 33:27).

It is my hope and prayer that through my family's story you have gained insight into your own situation and the lives of those close to you. While we probably cannot alter our children's decisions or the courses they choose, we may be able to make choices that will be supportive and positive in light of their decisions. We need to take responsibility for our actions, moving carefully and lovingly, remembering that acceptance of the divorce doesn't necessarily mean approval. It is possible to love our children even when circumstances require it to be tough love.

We can't see into the future, but we can seek to be a stable, ongoing presence, extending ourselves in love to our children and grandchildren. We can try to be available for them as the years and geography allow. The storms of life, in a variety of forms, come to us all. When we have built on the solid foundation of belief in God, we will be able to withstand those storms.

I realize that all of our stories are different. You may be totally cut off from your children or grandchildren and feel hopeless about the whole situation. You may find that extending yourself to others will be a healthy distraction and a way to ease your pain. There may be people or programs in your church or community that would greatly appreciate the gift of your time. Reaching out to single-parent families with Christian love and support can be very satisfying. Many have found that the act of giving brings fulfillment.

Please know that our Lord Jesus is with you to give comfort and counsel and to share your life. He is available to each one of us who turn to him; the Scripture makes this promise over and over again. "So do not fear, for I am with you; do not be dismayed, for I am your God. I will strengthen you and help you; I will uphold you with my righteous right hand" (Is 41:10); "I can do everything through him who gives me strength" (Phil 4:13). In all of our lives there are experiences of pain, but with Christ's love as a resource we can move beyond the pain in our quest for wholeness, understanding and love.

The Chinese word for *crisis* is written with two characters: the one for *danger* and the one for *opportunity*. Both are aspects of broken relationships. There are certainly danger, damage and despair when families experience divorce. But—once we catch our breath—there is also opportunity: the challenge of coping with change, the soul-stretching exercise of learning forgiveness, the healing and growth that come as we move ahead with God's help. Everyone in our family has had to examine what it means to love unconditionally. And we've had to explore how we can be more creative and godly in the midst of conflicting ideas and values.

Danger, yes. But opportunity as well. And it is true of your crisis too. With God's help you can survive it and become stronger through it.

Notes

Chapter 3: "I'm Angry, Worried and Afraid"

[1]Theodore Rubin, *The Angry Book* (New York: Macmillan/Collier, 1969), pp. 21-25.

[2]Michael Rogers, Presbyterian Counseling Service, Seattle, Wash. Personal interview, 1994.

[3]Lloyd Ogilvie, *Making Stress Work for You* (Waco, Tex.: Word, 1984), p. 171.

Chapter 4: But It's Time to Move On

[1]Eugene Peterson, *Run with the Horses* (Downers Grove, Ill.: InterVarsity Press, 1983), pp. 147-56.

[2]Ibid., p. 152.

[3]Sandra D. Wilson, *Shame-Free Parenting* (Downers Grove, Ill.: InterVarsity Press, 1992), p. 48.

[4]David Augsburger, *Caring Enough to Forgive* (Ventura, Calif.: Regal, 1981), p. 66.

[5]Peter Kreeft, *Making Choices* (Ann Arbor, Mich.: Servant Books, 1990), pp. 198-99.

Chapter 5: "How Can I Help My Hurting Child?"

[1]Dorothy W. Gottlieb, Inez B. Gottlieb and Marjorie A. Slavin, *What to Do When Your Son or Daughter Divorces* (New York: Bantam, 1988), p. 112.

Chapter 6: What About the Ex-Spouse—and the *New* One?

[1]Tim Dearborn, president of Seattle Association for Theological Education. Quoted from a 1993 lecture.

[2]Harold Ivan Smith, *Help for Parents of a Divorced Son or Daughter* (St. Louis, Mo.: Concordia Publishing House, 1981), p. 32.

[3]Ibid., p. 34.

Chapter 7: New Roles with Your Grandchildren

[1]Judith Wallerstein, *Second Chances* (New York: Ticknor and Fields, 1989), p. 60.

[2]Ibid., p. 61.

[3]Ibid., p. 62.

[4]Claire Ansberry, "Kids Are Often Losers in Joint Custody," *Wall Street*

Journal, Sept. 22, 1988, p. 39.

[5]Robert A. Aldrich and Glenn Austin, *Grandparenting for the Nineties* (San Marcos, Calif.: R. Erdmann, 1991), pp. 142-62. Paraphrased excerpts.

Chapter 9: Facing Embarrassing and Shameful Truths

[1]Debra L. Pearce, Roanoke Therapy Associates, Seattle, Wash. Material transcribed from taped interview, 1991.

[2]Ibid.

[3]Ibid.

[4]Ibid.

[5]Wilson, *Shame-Free Parenting,* pp. 205-7.

[6]Tim Snow, pastor, University Presbyterian Church, Seattle, Wash. Transcribed from taped interview, 1991.

[7]Bruce Larson. Transcribed from taped interview, 1991.

[8]Gerhard Hauer, *Longing for Tenderness: Responsible Love Before Marriage* (Downers Grove, Ill.: InterVarsity Press, 1983), pp. 111-32.

[9]Larson, taped interview.

[10]Ibid.

Chapter 11: The Church's Response

[1]John Stott, *Marriage and Divorce* (Downers Grove, Ill.: InterVarsity Press, 1985), pp. 3-4.

[2]H. Wayne House, ed., *Divorce and Remarriage: Four Christian Views* (Downers Grove, Ill.: InterVarsity Press, 1990).

[3]For information, write Stephen Ministries, 8011 Dale, St. Louis, MO 63117-1449. Phone (314) 645-5511.

Chapter 12: Gaining Perspective Through Small Groups

[1]Tresa Wilbee Wiggins, "Divorce and the Extended Family Member: What About Me?" Seattle Pacific University, unpublished master's thesis, 1985. Paraphrased excerpts.

For Further Reading

Understanding Divorce

Smith, Harold Ivan. *I Wish Someone Understood My Divorce*. Minneapolis: Augsburg, 1981.

Parents can learn from this book and perhaps offer it to their children. Helps the divorcing individual come to terms with his or her situation, overcome common fears, set priorities for living and discover resources for healing, growth and renewal of faith.

Wallerstein, Judith. *Second Chances: Men, Women and Children a Decade After Divorce*. New York: Ticknor and Fields, 1989.

A comprehensive and immensely readable look at the life-changing impact of divorce on the family.

Blended Families and Stepfamilies

Bustanoby, Andre. *The Readymade Family: How to Be a Stepparent and Survive*. Grand Rapids, Mich.: Zondervan, 1982.

"It is crucial that stepparents understand how to use their circumstances wisely to meet the need for love, security, and acceptance everyone craves."

Reed, Bobbie. *Stepfamilies: Living in Christian Harmony*. St. Louis: Concordia, 1980.

Gives sound, intelligent advice that will help your stepfamily be a healthy and vigorous Christian family.

Visher, Emily B., and John S. Visher. *Stepfamilies: A Guide to Working with Stepparents and Stepchildren*. New York: Brunner-Mazel, 1979.

Virginia Satir says of the book, "There is no reason why a stepfamily cannot be a first-class place for bringing up children and also helping adults involved to live creatively. Instead of approaching living in a stepfamily as a make-do situation, it can become a creative challenge for a new life for everybody. . . . Useful to counselors, pastors, parents, stepparents and teachers. The more people who understand about this, the more possible will be a nurturing environment in which the new family can get societal support."

Books of Inspiration and Understanding
Hansel, Tim. *You Gotta Keep Dancin'*. Elgin, Ill.: Cook, 1986.
  Presents the opportunity to be transformed by our suffering as we choose to move in one direction or the other.
Keller, Phillip. *A Shepherd Looks at Psalm 23*. Grand Rapids, Mich.: Zondervan, 1970.
  A look at one of the best-loved psalms from the perspective of an experienced shepherd. The reader will be encouraged by the expressions of loving care that Jesus offers those who follow him.
Larson, Bruce. *There's a Lot More to Health Than Not Being Sick*. Waco, Tex.: Word, 1981.
  After lengthy research, Larson shows that the choices we make can contribute to our wellness: choices to stop blaming others for our problems, to make solid friendships, to live by creative risk and to be excited about the future.
L'Engle, Madeleine. *A Circle of Quiet*. New York: Seabury, 1972.
  A candid personal look at the life of a writer who has inspired many. Sharing her world will enlarge your understanding and your faith in God.
  _____. *The Irrational Season*. New York: Seabury, 1979.
  An uplifting walk through the Christian year with L'Engle as a professional woman, wife, mother and grandmother.
Tournier, Paul. *To Understand Each Other*. Atlanta: John Knox Press, 1967.
  The ability to understand each other, particularly in times of family stress, is what counts in working out marital happiness. Tournier suggests ways to achieve this understanding.

General Understanding
Aldrich, Robert A., and Glenn Austin. *Grandparenting for the Nineties*. San Marcos, Calif.: R. Erdmann, 1991.
  We can greatly enlarge the impact we have as elders, custodians of wisdom and teachers of solid values. The wisdom distilled in this book offers us hope and help in pulling our families closer together.

Journaling
Ranier, Tristine. *The New Diary: How to Use a Journal for Self-Guidance and Expanded Creativity*. Los Angeles: Jeremy P. Tarcher, 1978.
  Helpful information about using your diary or journal to expand your ability to observe, grow in self-awareness, work through your emotions, clarify goals and visualize the future.
Smith, Margaret D. *Journal Keeper*. Grand Rapids, Mich.: Eerdmans, 1992.
  Encouragement for beginning a journal journey with yourself, opening your heart with God to experience *shalom*—a sense of wholeness and well-being.

CREATE AND CELEBRATE YOUR CHURCH'S UNIQUENESS

LINCOLN CHRISTIAN COLLEGE AND SEMINARY

Books by Harold J. Westing

Create and Celebrate Your Church's Uniqueness

Evaluate and Grow

I'd Love to Tell the Story

The Multiple Church-staff Handbook

*Super Superintendent: A Layman's Guide to
Sunday School Management*